Somebody's Son

Val & Bev Savage

*Proceeds from the sale of this book will be donated to
Mill Grove, formerly a children's home and now a residential
community that features prominently in the story*

ISBN: 978-1-78808-870-1

The authors have tried to recreate events, locales and conversations from memories of them and the accounts of others. The authors have made every effort to recall conversations and events accurately but they do not assume and hereby disclaim any liability to any party for any loss, damage or disruption caused by errors or omissions resulting from negligence, accident or any other cause. In order to maintain their anonymity in some instances the authors have changed the names of individuals and places. They may have changed some identifying characteristics and details such as physical properties, occupations and places of residence.

Commendations

This book is a marvellous testimony to what God can do with a broken life placed into His hands. It has all the elements of a gripping drama: secrets, conflicts, and mystery; love, loyalty and loss; hopes, fears and a rugged persevering faith.

For several years, Val Savage deployed her sleuthing and scribing skills to uncover and piece together the moving and inspiring story you are about to enjoy. Fast paced and well-written, 'Somebody's Son' reads like a novel, made more compelling because it is all true. Get ready for an emotional journey that will take you through pain and sorrow and leave you with a sense of wonder at the redeeming grace of God.

To know Bev Savage is to admire the unusual depth of his wisdom, the robust strength of his faith and the abundant fruitfulness of his ministry. Throughout his life, Bev has modelled an intense desire to know more of God, and a relentless perseverance in the work that God has called him to pursue.

People who see this may wonder, 'Where did it come from?' As you are about to discover, Bev's early years might easily have led to a life of dysfunction. But God laid hold on him and made him the godly pastor, Christ-exalting preacher and visionary leader, for whom many are so deeply thankful.

Bev's extraordinary story is told here with insight and candour without a hint of self-pity or pride. Reading this book will renew your hope and bring joy to your heart. If you carry heavy burdens it will help you to persevere. If you have suffered deep wounds it will help you to forgive. But most of all, Bev's story will give you a fresh glimpse of how God works in all things for the good of those who love Him, and of what His redeeming grace might yet do for you.

Colin S. Smith, BA, Theology; M.Phil, London Bible College
Senior Pastor, The Orchard, Chicago, www.theorchardefc.org
President, Unlocking the Bible, www.unlockingthebible.org

I had the privilege of being present when Bev preached his remarkable sermon in Tiptree United Reformed Church in May 2000, mentioned in chapter 3, a sermon that kick-started the journey of self-discovery charted in this book. Val spoke with me after the service and told me that she knew he had needed to preach it for many years. Little did she or I know where things would then lead!

I also had the privilege of spending a day with Bev and Val in the USA shortly before Val died. Their love for each other was palpable, and there was no doubt that the writing of this life-story was a joint project made possible by their mutual love and their experience of God's love for them.

So it is that this compelling, honest and moving book is part of a bigger and living story in which God continues His work in Christ by the power of the Holy Spirit of reconciling the world to Himself.

Keith White, M.A, M.Phil, Ph.D.
Director of Mill Grove, www.millgrove.org.uk

Somebody's Son reads like a script for the immensely popular TV series, Who do you think you are? The difference here is that the real celebrity is God Himself. It gives the lie to the accepted wisdom that 'hurt people hurt people', as the grace of the Lord Jesus breaks the cycle of child neglect and abandonment. A candid, tangled, fascinating detective story, lovingly researched by a wife, herself afflicted by mental and physical illness, but determined that her 'man' would find his roots and lay any family skeletons at the one place where they can be buried without bitterness, the Cross of Christ. Fascinating and delightful!

Steve Brady PhD
Principal Moorlands College, Christchurch, UK.
www.moorlands.ac.uk

Contents

Acknowledgments

My wife, Ann, has shown immense understanding and generosity of spirit as she has supported me in completing this project. I am particularly indebted to Philip, Ian and Kate, and to my sister Sheila, without whose permission and encouragement this book could never have been published.

My friends, Colin and Karen Smith have been my constant companions, advisors and encouragers over many years. The part they have played in the production of this book has been invaluable.

My thanks also to Keith White who has advised and supported me out of his encyclopaedic knowledge of the history of Mill Grove and his personal acquaintance with its vast, ever-expanding family.

Many others have also offered their encouragement and advice for which I am very grateful.

SOMEBODY'S SON

Dedicated to our grandchildren -

Oliver and Christopher
Emily and Annie
Max and Joe

INTRODUCTION

Just before Easter 2016 Justin Welby, the 60 year old 105th Archbishop of Canterbury, discovered that the person whom he had always regarded as his father was not, in fact, a biological relative. A former editor of the Daily Telegraph, Charles Moore, broke the news to him – and it came as a terrible shock. It transpired that his mother, Lady Williams of Elvel, had a liaison with Sir Winston Churchill's last private secretary, the late Sir Anthony Montague Brown, just before she married in 1955. Justin was born in January 1956.

For all his privileged upbringing, Justin's life was deeply affected by the alcoholism of Gavin Welby and Jane, his mother. Yet, as their public statements revealed, their story is not one of hopelessness but of redemption. Their family and their faith helped her to overcome her alcoholism, and Justin to demonstrate that a difficult start in life can be faced and overcome. In Justin's words, "I know that I find who I am in Jesus Christ, not in genetics. My identity in Him never changes …" Although there are elements of sadness, and even tragedy in my father's (Gavin Welby) case, this is a story of redemption and hope from a place of tumultuous difficulty and near despair in several lives."

Justin Welby's words could well sum up my own story. It would never have been told had it not been for my late wife's commitment to researching its details and presenting the complicated story in an intelligible form. I started out as a somewhat reluctant participant in her project but lovingly Val led me by the hand into the unexplored world of my early years, helped me come to terms with its revelations and, eventually, to celebrate my own experience of redemption and hope.

What follows is a biography written by Val with a covering of my more recent autobiographical recollections and reflections. It is more than a chronological account. It is a description of a journey of discovery, a treasure hunt. It resembles a detective story as it unearths facts and reveals clues along the way which lead to unexpected encounters and surprising conclusions. You are invited to experience the twists and turns of the journey in much the same way as we did and, when all is said and done, to find that you are left with unanswered questions and tantalisingly unexplored areas of interest just as we were, territory that is now beyond our reach. That's life!

Val and I agreed that we would leave this account for our family, if for no one else, so that successive generations would know of their ancestry and always have reason to think about the goodness of God to us.

We also felt then, and I feel now a sense of responsibility to tell this story more widely because, the undeserved grace of God that has followed me all my life, should be known and celebrated. My experience is far from unique since what He has done for me He has done for millions of others across the world and throughout the ages, for all those people who have found their identity in Christ. We simply add our testimony to millions of others who tell the same story of the love of Christ for them.

Val died in November 2006 and three years later I married Ann whom we had known for many years. For ten years after her death, Val's manuscript has been locked away in a drawer in my office like a meal carefully prepared and frozen for future use. I always knew that one day I would need to bring it out, taste it again for myself and serve it up.

The legacy of a poor start in life will always leave its mark but now at 77 years of age I am able to look back with the mellow perspective of older years, with deep appreciation for all who have influenced me for good and with somewhat bewildered devotion to my heavenly Father who chose to rescue me when I was very young and has kept me in His care ever since.

Every effort has been made to be accurate in relating the facts, only changing some names to protect those who are still living.

Bournemouth 2017

SOMEBODY'S SON

Part 1
NOW AND THEN

Though my father and mother forsake me,
the Lord will receive me
Psalm 27:10

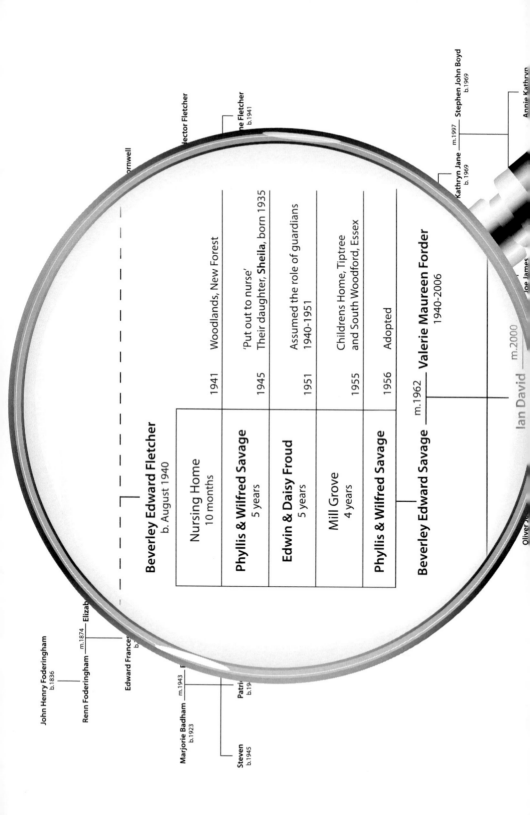

Hector Fletcher

...ne Fletcher
b.1941

...ornwell

Beverley Edward Fletcher
b. August 1940

Nursing Home 10 months	1941	Woodlands, New Forest
Phyllis & Wilfred Savage 5 years	1945	'Put out to nurse' Their daughter, **Sheila**, born 1935
Edwin & Daisy Froud 5 years	1951	Assumed the role of guardians 1940-1951
Mill Grove 4 years	1955	Childrens Home, Tiptree and South Woodford, Essex
Phyllis & Wilfred Savage	1956	Adopted

Beverley Edward Savage —— m.1962 —— **Valerie Maureen Forder**
1940-2006

Kathryn Jane —— m.1997 —— **Stephen John Boyd**
b.1969   b.1969

Annie Kathryn

Ian David —— m.2000 ——

Joe James

Oliver ...

John Henry Foderingham
b.1836

Renn Foderingham —— m.1874 —— Elizab...

Edward Frances...

Marjorie Badham —— m.1943 —— Patri...
b.1923   b.19...

Steven
b.1945

> *I know that I find who I am in Jesus Christ, not in genetics. My identity in Him never changes.*
> Justin Welby

Chapter 1
GATHERED FACTS

"Well, what are you expecting to find?" I asked as Bev, my husband, and I neared the end of our journey.

"Oh, nothing much," he said, "Maybe a few letters and forms – a cover story. There can't be much more than that can there?"

The M25 circular motorway around London, South East England, is one of the busiest in the country. We used it regularly at that time, although never for pleasure, so as we negotiated our way through the heavy traffic that overcast June morning, we were glad to have other things to occupy our minds. Our destination was usually the Croydon office of the Fellowship of Independent Evangelical Churches (FIEC), which Bev visited regularly as part of his work, or one of the several committee rooms, churches or conference centres with which he was so familiar. But today our destination was very different. We were visiting a children's home.

Mill Grove
Although it now stands within sight and sound of an elevated and imposing road intersection on the outskirts of east London, 'Mill Grove' still nestles

comfortably into the bank beside Crescent Road, a modest Victorian terrace-lined street in suburban South Woodford. It has been there for well over a century. We had visited it many times, more so since Bev had become a Trustee of the Home. Within its archives are records that relate to over 1000 children who have passed through its care, but today there was just one file that interested us. Bev had been taken into the home as a ten year old child, and it was his file that we were travelling to see. In the decades of adult life that followed his time in care, it had never occurred to him to find out what lay buried there until now, the 24th June 2000, just a few weeks before his sixtieth birthday. At his own request he and I would examine his file for the first time.

Over the years I had gathered enough information about his background to become fascinated by what might lie hidden behind the somewhat incoherent surface details. He seemed not to care about his roots but I did and, since I had always loved research, he made a perfect subject for me to investigate.

With his head full of his work, he was largely unaware of what I was doing, but from time to time I would surprise him by telling him of a discovery I had made about one or other of his relatives. He was always curious, but the conversation soon moved on to other more pressing topics. This was my project. He seemed fine with that, as long as it didn't demand anything of him. However, today as we travelled towards Mill Grove, he was fully engaged and we were both more anxious than we cared to admit.

I had looked forward to this journey for over a year. I was coming close to exhausting my leads and I hoped to find new ones. What new information we might discover from the file I had no idea. Maybe all I could reasonably expect to find was confirmation of the basic facts that I had already gathered.

The Facts

Born – 14th August 1940 in a Nursing Home in a quiet corner of the New Forest in Hampshire, Central Southern England.

Registered – Beverley Edward Fletcher, the son of Hector and Lilian Fletcher.

We already knew that his birth certificate was a fabrication. His father was in fact a single man, Edward Cyril Foderingham, known to his friends as 'Foddy' or Ted. He was lodging with a Mr Edwin and Mrs Winifred (Daisy) Froud when the child was conceived. Ted was an insurance agent with the Liverpool Victoria Friendly Society which offered access to financial products sold by agents who went door-to-door collecting premiums and building relationships with customers. Ted Foderingham went from door to door building relationships with customers - some of which became the subject of village gossip.

Circumstances – immediately following his birth he was left in the Nursing Home.

He was there for some months. It seemed likely that it was Daisy Froud, Ted's landlady, who made arrangements to 'put him out to nurse' with a Mr and Mrs Savage. Daisy had come to know the Savages when she took on Ted's insurance round after he was called up to serve in the Royal Air Force. The Savages were among his clients.

First five years – he lived with Phyllis and Wilfred Savage and their daughter, Sheila, who was six years old when he arrived. They loved him and treated him as their own son.

They were told that Beverley was the child of Ted's brother or cousin who had been killed in the war. They suspected this was not the whole story but they could gather no more information about

> *We already knew his birth certificate was a fabrication*

him or what became of his mother. Only much later did they discover the truth that he was, in fact, Ted Foderingham's own son and that his mother, Lilian Fletcher, was married to the Manager of the Winchester office of the Liverpool Victoria Friendly Society.

From 5 to 10 – the war ended in 1945 and Ted was demobbed and returned to his insurance round. Daisy, finding herself free to pursue a life of her own choosing again, decided that the time had come for her to care for the child. And so one day without warning she took him from the Savages to live with her and Edwin in a large, well-appointed bungalow in Chandlers Ford, an affluent suburb of Eastleigh, a railway town midway between Winchester and Southampton. From then on Edwin and Daisy Froud seem to have assumed responsibility for the 'orphan' and they gave him their name.

Meanwhile, Ted Foderingham married in November 1943 and two years later took his young wife, Marjorie, to live with him alongside the Frouds in the bungalow where he had been a lodger. There, over the next few years, Ted and Marjorie had three children, a son and two daughters.

It was into this environment that Daisy Froud suddenly introduced Bev. Whatever her motives, her action brought misery to the entire household – including the boy, a situation made much worse when a few years later Daisy's health began to deteriorate. It gradually became obvious that she would not be able to continue to care for the child and so his future became a serious problem for them all.

From 10 to 15 – following an increasingly desperate search for somewhere to place him, and just a few weeks after Daisy Froud's death, the ten year old was admitted to Mill Grove, then called 'The Children's Home and Mission', in April 1951.

15 – he left school and Mill Grove and returned to live with Mr & Mrs Savage. Edwin Froud having also died, Bev asked Phyllis and Wilfred Savage if they would become his parents, a request to which they readily acceded. He was formally adopted by them in February 1956.

These facts were already familiar to us.

SOMEBODY'S SON

Chapter 2

THE FILE

As we turned into Crescent Road, the familiar sight of the two imposing semi-detached three storied Victorian houses appeared dead ahead. Numbers 8 and 10 have a commanding view of the road with their basements nestling almost out of sight below the bank. Our eye followed the line of two short flights of stone steps that climb to adjacent front doors on the first floor of each house, and to the text above them. It was a quote from the Bible that was particularly popular in Victorian times when the home was founded. Then the British Empire was in the ascendency and Christian mission was expanding. 'Have faith in God' it proclaimed.

We drove past the halls and houses in which the staff and children lived and stopped outside the place that had become a refuge for many children and families in need, and to Bev 50 years previously. We climbed the steps to number 10 to receive the customary warm welcome from Ruth, the Director's wife. Her friendliness was particularly reassuring that day. She quietened our nerves, at least briefly, as we talked animatedly and exchanged news. It took just a few minutes to adjust to being back in the 'family' atmosphere again. For all the sadness that surrounds children and families in need, Mill Grove is a place where many have learned to relax and smile again as they begin to enjoy release from the pressures of dysfunctional people and difficult circumstances.

Eventually, a natural break in the conversation led to us being shown to a small pleasant sitting room overlooking a large lawn at the rear of the house. A tray of tea was placed thoughtfully beside us and we were left alone with Bev's file in our hands.

Correspondence

We opened its blue cover and found the contents neatly assembled in reverse chronological order. First, we came to the most recent correspondence between us and 'The Mill Grove Family'. Once a year at least, around Christmas time, we would write to update our family and friends with our news and concerns and ask them to pray for us. A copy of our letter always went to Mill Grove and we in turn received greetings from the Family. Each of our letters was carefully saved in the file.

Turning the pages we came next to correspondence written by Bev during his late 'teens and early twenties telling in turn of his growing sense of calling to become a Christian Minister, of our engagement, our wedding and the birth of our first son.

Next came letters written soon after he had left the Home, letters that he was too embarrassed to read aloud. "They sound horribly 'preachy'", he said, "and the spelling's not so hot either!" He seemed to be going so slowly and our time was limited. I was impatient to get back to the beginning so I encouraged him to move on more quickly.

I watched in silence as the pages slowly turned. Then he paused to read a hand written letter from Edwin Froud that clearly affected him. He began to read it to me. "Beverley's father practically ignores him, although they are living in our home ..." He began to breathe heavily fighting for control. There in black and white he read for himself words that were written fifty years earlier that spelled out clearly how he had been regarded by his own father whom he saw every day – indeed, with whom he lived.

To his surprise, and mine, that revelation produced an almost uncontrollable upsurge of emotion in him that surfaced without warning. The well-rehearsed skeletal details of his early life were suddenly clothed with flesh – and it hurt, it hurt a lot.

I reached out to him as he struggled. We seemed to sit in silence for a long time, he just couldn't move on. We were both relieved when Ruth arrived to rescue us. We asked if we might take the file away to copy its contents. "It's yours to keep", she said, and so we left carrying it with us to read slowly in the quiet of our own home where no one could see the effect those ancient documents produced.

Centenary Celebration

I could only recall one occasion when Bev had shown any emotion about his past in all the forty five years that I had known and loved him. It was just six

> The well-rehearsed skeletal details of his early life were suddenly clothed with flesh – and it hurt, it hurt a lot

weeks previously when we attended Mill Grove's Centenary celebration.

One of the great traditions of the home is its annual event held in May and known as 'Our Day'. Then many former 'family members', supporters and friends gather for a service of thanksgiving, a grand reunion and a tour of the buildings and gardens that hundreds experienced as their first secure 'home'. Parents and grandparents delight to show their children and grandchildren where they used to sleep and play and familiar stories are retold, like that of the rent man who brought his own rent and the bakers van that broke down outside the home when there was nothing inside to eat. They are often related with a wonder like that of the first time of telling.

An extraordinary family

Mill Grove really is an extraordinary 'family' that has changed the lives of hundreds of children for good but remarkably it has done so with very little publicity or visible means of support. It was established in 1899 by an outstanding Christian evangelist by the name of Herbert White. He was supported by his wife, Edith, and 'Ma Hutchins', a single lady who became 'mother' to hundreds of children in need. At the beginning it was called the 'Home for Destitute and Motherless Children' and had three clear objectives –

1. To receive destitute or needy children.
2. To bring children to know the Lord Jesus Christ as their Saviour.
3. To prove that God is able to answer prayer by appealing to Him alone for workers, funds and even every day needs such as food.

A focus of attention

As might be expected, this last objective has attracted considerable attention over the years of its existence, and it still does today. It largely accounts for the fact that the work of Mill Grove and its amazing history is not widely known since the very principles on which it was founded and still operates keeps it out of the press, even the Christian press.

Understandably, such an approach raises concerns. In a world where faith is often derided, especially the Christian faith, people frequently arrive at Mill Grove curious and somewhat sceptical about its history and its approach to life. Politicians, civil servants, inspectors, social workers and specialist child-care professionals, as well as members of the general public, visit to find out for themselves if it could really be true that prayer and faith in God alone could sustain such a demanding work.

Many with little or no faith leave bemused by what they witness. Mill Grove is an anomaly to them. Unable to accept the Christian principles on which it was founded, they are at a loss to explain how it is that, well over 100 years after it came into being, it continues to serve generously everyone who comes within its orbit.

For Christian visitors, on the other hand, it remains an irrefutable testimony to the faithfulness of a present and living God who cares for those who trust him and it continues to be a profound inspiration to the faith of countless numbers of people scattered around the world.

Proof of the Being of God

Dr D Martin Lloyd-Jones, the renowned Minister of Westminster Chapel, London, and a leading evangelical of the 20th century, took a personal interest in Mill Grove. He was a close friend of

> In a world where faith is often derided, people arrive at Mill Grove curious and sceptical about its history and approach.

Herbert White the founder, and conducted his funeral. He once said of him, "I always like to meet a great man and to listen to a great man and I was one of those who was in a sense ... a hero-worshipper of our friend Mr Herbert White."*

On another occasion he commented, "A work like this is a proof in and of itself of the Being of God. You cannot explain the astonishing miracles and happenings that have taken place in connection with it, the wonderful answers to prayer – they cannot be explained adequately, and in any other terms, apart from the Being of God."**

Incidentally 'The Doctor', as he was universally known, was later to play a significant part in our lives too as you will discover.

Near this spot stood "The Grove" (formerly Windmill Hall) where members of the Mill Grove family lived throughout the Second World War. Intended as a Convalescent Home, it proved to be a timely safe place when the home at Woodford (The Childrens' Home & Mission) was closed due to enemy air raids on London. Mill Grove was founded in 1899, as a work of faith trusting in God, by Herbert White and Rosa Hutchin. This plaque was erected by some of the children who lived at The Grove as a token of their affection and appreciation to those who lovingly cared for them.

8TH MAY 2011

www.millgrove.org.uk

HAVE FAITH IN GOD · MARK 11.22

*Not Like Any Other Home, Bob Holman 1994 *p. 131 **p. 62*

Tiptree memories

'Our Day' in the year 2000 was a celebration of
a century of God's faithfulness. Former 'family
members' and friends made a special effort to be
present, some travelling half way around the world.

Bev was invited to preach on the Sunday morning
of that weekend, not in Woodford where the Home
had been located from the beginning, but in a United
Reformed Church in Tiptree, an Essex village some
two hours away. It was to this village that staff
and children were evacuated during WW2, to 'The
Grove', a large gracious Victorian double-fronted
house located on a main road into the village.

Bev was formally received into the Home in the
Woodford headquarters, but was immediately
transferred to Tiptree where he spent his first year in
care. During that year fewer and fewer children were
placed there and The Grove closed altogether the
following summer. He, along with the few remaining
residents, was then transferred to Woodford. The
Grove was sold in 1954 and demolished in the 1990s
when a supermarket was erected on the site. Today
the only evidence that it ever existed is a plaque on a
wall adjoining the supermarket car park.

Its memory is also kept alive by its inclusion
alongside that of 'The Mill', an area now engulfed by
multi-lane highways a short distance from Crescent
Road, in the title 'Mill Grove'. As we drove through
the village that Sunday morning of the Centenary
Celebration and neared the church, Bev began to
share memories that I had not heard before.

Chapter 3

AWAKENING

As General Secretary of the FIEC at this time, Bev was preaching most Sundays in one or other of over four hundred affiliated churches throughout Britain, but this engagement was quite different. He had not been looking forward to it – but that was nothing new. It puzzled us both that he seemed ill at ease when we visited Mill Grove.

He was well aware of the debt he owed to generations of the White family and their helpers for their outstanding dedication to helping children like him, but he was always strangely reluctant to stay long. Perhaps it was little more than the reaction of some adult children when they visit their childhood home and their parents, but I sensed that there was more to it than that.

Private world

For all his outgoing friendliness, he finds close relationships difficult to handle. He moves on from people and situations much more easily than me. Mum Savage confided to me near the end of her life that, for all their love for each other, he sometimes seemed distant, almost secretive. I knew exactly what she meant. I had experienced it myself and had many

I wished I lived in a house in a tree that nobody knew about but me; I'd have a door and paint it brown with a little rope ladder to pull up and down.

opportunities to watch and listen as he encouraged people to confide in him as a Pastor, which they usually did with ease, but only very rarely did he reveal details about himself.

So, I suppose that I should not have been surprised that my research into his life would seem to him an unwelcome intrusion into his very private world.

He had many reasons to distrust the people around him as a child, of course, and he often imagined a life free from adults. One of his favourite poems as a child began, 'I wished I lived in a house in a tree that nobody knew about but me; I'd have a door and I'd paint it brown with a little rope ladder to pull up and down.' He would sometimes lie awake trying to work out how he could live in woods on his own and survive without detection. How would he disguise the tree house and the smoke from the chimney? Where could he obtain food and escape the attention of inquisitive grown- ups?

But childhood fantasies seem to have turned into a lifelong habit of concealing his history and his inner thoughts. What accounted for that, nature or nurture? I couldn't tell but interestingly one of our sons shows similar traits.

Very few people who have known Bev Savage over the years would guess that he had such a troubled start to life. Actually his reluctance to share information about himself has been an asset to him in his role as a minister since, as Dr D M Lloyd -Jones preached at our service of introduction to our second church, it is a requirement of a Pastor not to preach himself but "Christ Jesus as Lord."

The sermon

He stood before a very full church that morning in Tiptree. Normally articulate and relaxed, words did not come easily. The text he had chosen to speak on was from Genesis chapter 50 verse 20.

The chapter tells the story of a man named Joseph who was once abused and sold into slavery by his brothers. Many years later, when he occupied a position of high authority in Egypt, Joseph's brothers came asking for his help. They did not recognise him at first, but when eventually they did, they feared that he would exact revenge on them for all he had suffered because of them. Instead Joseph responded to them by saying something entirely unexpected, "You intended to harm me but God intended it for good, to accomplish what is now being done, the saving of many lives."

There were many in the congregation that day who had been victims of circumstances beyond their control and of other people's poor behaviour. Some had been abandoned, neglected and abused in childhood; others had been orphaned. Many had discovered already that faith in Jesus Christ could turn their pain and sadness into something very positive, but not all.

Bev spoke of the way in which he was able to trace a pattern of God's goodness in his own life and ended by speaking to those who might see themselves as victims. "There is no future in seeing ourselves that way", he said. "A troubled childhood does not have to blight the whole of life. The love that God has for us can rescue us."

It was not a new thought, of course. Many had made the point before him and since – and in more striking language. Rabbi Jonathan Sacks, for example, put it well. "The flight from responsibility into victimhood is the oldest of all human temptations... But it is negative, destructive ... It leads us to the impotence of anger and the anger of impotence. The best way of curing a victim is to help him cease to think of himself as a victim."*

> A troubled childhood does not have to blight the whole of life.

Bev had never once spoken of himself as a victim or appeared to think of himself that way. In fact, he seemed never to have thought about his past at all, had not once looked squarely in the face of his own history, had always moved on, kept moving on without looking back. It had become the habit of his life.

As I struggled to make a connection between what he preached that day in Tiptree, and the way in which he was evidently moved as he spoke, one thing became clear, this was a sermon he had needed to preach for a long time and it awakened something within him that left him feeling emotionally drained.

The village school

After the service I was in my element gathering vivid impressions of what it had been like to live in the Home from those who had experienced it first-hand. Tiptree village school was opened for us to visit and a young member of staff welcomed us and showed us round. We toured the classrooms and enjoyed a display of old photographs. As we made our way slowly around the buildings, Bev and his friends shared their memories of what it was like to be at the school, recalling the aptly named Mr Butcher who was an expert at wielding a Stool Ball bat as a deterrent to breaking the rules.

Among the various records we found a punishment book. There recorded was 'Geoffrey - running in the corridor' and other equally serious misdemeanours.

Looking through the school log book Bev hit on the record of the death of his new friend with whom he had been playing when he was instantly killed just a few feet from him. He ran blindly under the wheels of a delivery lorry which was slowly winding its way through the crowded playground to the school kitchen. He recalled the floods of the winter of 1952 which had been particularly bad in Canvey Island, Essex, where the boy had been buried. This preyed on his mind at the time as he imagined the boy's body being washed away and being lost for ever.

> I feel like howling for a week and I don't know why

That weekend we met people whom Bev hadn't seen for almost fifty years and I listened intently as they shared their stories and reminisced together until eventually they said their goodbyes, knowing that they were unlikely ever to meet again. We had visited Woodford many times over the years but this return to Tiptree triggered memories that had long been buried.

As we made our way home that evening he suddenly confided, "I feel like howling for a week and I don't know why".

SOMEBODY'S SON

Chapter 4

ALIVE?

In addition to my fascination with Bev's personal story, I was motivated in my quest for information by the conviction that it was important that our three children, all now in their thirties and married and with children of their own, should know more about their ancestry, to know what was in their genes and, if possible, to know about our family's medical history. We were all intrigued, for example, by the fact that we had a blond, blue-eyed daughter and a son who quickly turns an enviable bronze colour in the sun.

These differences had been a topic of light-hearted conversation and speculation over the years, especially when the boys introduced their girlfriends into the family. Naturally, they were inquisitive about our background, but their questions were always answered with more humour than fact because we knew so little.

More questions than answers

As I examined Bev's file at my leisure in the weeks following our visit to Mill Grove, certain questions began to crystalize in my mind. I wasn't at all sure that we would ever be able to find answers to them, but they were important enough to occupy my thoughts.

The earliest black and white photograph we have of Bev shows him in a garden outside the French doors of a large house in the arms of a uniformed nurse. The foliage is thin on the surrounding trees; it appears to be springtime. He had been born in August, so how did he come to be in the arms of a nurse in the spring? Did his natural mother abandon him? Did no one claim him as theirs? Surely, if he was still in the nursing home several months after his birth, his care did not come without cost; so who paid for it?

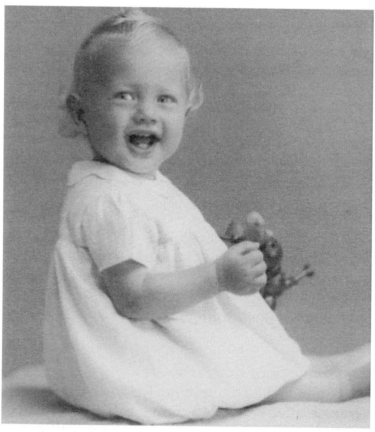

As I thought of his birth mother I tried to imagine

what kind of relationship she had had with Ted Foderingham and how Hector, her husband, had reacted to news of her pregnancy and to the realisation that it was one of his employees who was responsible. What part did he play in the decision for the child to be born in a nursing home in the New Forest some twenty miles away from Winchester where I assumed they lived?

Beverley

Then, who chose to name him 'Beverley', a name that has caused him considerable embarrassment all his life. He has often said that he wished that he had changed it when he was adopted but with three 'mothers' - Daisy Froud, Phyllis Savage, and the unknown Lilian Fletcher, and three 'fathers' – Ted Foderingham, Edwin Froud and Wilfred Savage, his Christian name at least provided some continuity to his identity.

An appalling decision

Then again, whatever possessed fifty year old Daisy Froud to think that she could take on responsibility for a five year old and have him live with her and her husband in the same bungalow in which Ted and Marjorie lived with their children?

The Savages loved him dearly and had formed a deep bond with him. Why weren't they allowed to keep him? He was never accepted as part of the Foderingham family or allowed to play with their children but instead confined to the Frouds' area of the bungalow. He became the whipping boy for everything that went wrong between them.

In removing him from the secure and loving environment of the Savage family and taking him to join the dysfunctional household in Chandlers Ford, Daisy made an appalling decision with awful

> With three 'mothers' and three 'fathers' his Christian name at least provided some continuity to his identity.

> Sometimes fishing in the village pond results in pulling out relics of the past that, in retrospect, we wished had remained hidden.

consequences for everyone living there, including herself.

Bev recalls being known by the surname 'Froud' before he entered the children's home, although it transpired that at no time had the Frouds officially adopted him or, as far as we knew, been made his legal guardians.

No reason to stop now

I soon realised that, instead of the two of us being familiar with his history, there were some very significant gaps in our knowledge.

For the first time he began to show some interest in my research. He was working very long hours and constantly travelling the country at this time and remained nervous about what I was discovering in his absence and where the search might take us. So we talked it through on several occasions and eventually decided to edge forward gently allowing time to share each new discovery and its implications before I did anything further with it.

For me it was an objective and fascinating treasure hunt and, in my enthusiasm to probe deeper into his past, I was not fully aware of the effect it was having on him. I recall asking myself one day whether it really would do much good to sift through his history in detail. Maybe too much time had elapsed for anything positive to come from it.

I remembered a remark once made by a doctor in connection with my own past, "Sometimes", he said, "fishing in the village pond results in pulling out relics of the past that, in retrospect, we wished had remained hidden." But now that we had an understanding of how we would proceed, and Bev was relatively willing for me to continue at least for the present, I saw no reason to stop. And there were new teasing leads to keep me interested.

Birth certificate

I sent for a copy of his original birth certificate. We
had known little about his birth mother, Lilian, but
the certificate revealed that she was twenty-nine
years old when she gave birth to him – not just a
youngster then. It also confirmed what we had read
in his file that her husband, Hector, had registered
himself as the baby's father, a generous act to protect
his wife's reputation, I thought.

By now she would be eighty-nine years old and
her husband well into his nineties. From that we
assumed that it was most likely that they would
both be dead, beyond reach and unaffected by any
enquiries we might make.

Visit to Andover

By chance I heard that an elderly woman named
'Fletcher' had been killed in a road traffic accident in
the Andover area of Hampshire. So I rang hospitals
and contacted newspapers and funeral directors to
find out more details but could find no record of the
incident.

The town of Andover was some forty five miles
from our home in Wiltshire so a few months later, on
one of Bev's days off, we travelled there to see if we
could gather any further information.

On a whim we went to view the Electoral Roll
for the district and were startled to read the names
of both Hector and Lilian Fletcher recorded there.
Unless they had died since the records were updated
the previous year, they were both still living just a
few streets away from where we were standing.

It took us several minutes to take in the
implications of this discovery. Bev suddenly said, "I
feel as if I'm being sucked down into some kind of
vortex." – a tad dramatic perhaps, but nonetheless
revealing of his continued nervousness about what

> **It would surely be unthinkable to disturb them in their advanced old age.**

we were doing. I tried to reassure him. "Look, this is not out of your control; you can stop this search any time you choose. We don't have to go any further with this."

But we both knew that it would take something quite extraordinary to stop us now.

Within those walls

We left the Registry Office and drove the few streets to the address recorded in the Electoral Roll. Parking across the road from the house, we stared at it in silence while we took in all its details and searched for clues about its occupants. It was a spacious, pleasant double fronted detached house sitting in its own well stocked grounds in a quiet road of similar properties. Its once bright white walls and blue painted windows and front door looked dull and somewhat neglected, typical of properties inhabited by the very elderly.

Behind those walls, we imagined, rested a couple who once played the most significant part in determining the course of Bev's life. We were actually within reach of the woman who had been a shadowy figure in my thoughts for many years. Whatever would they think if they knew that we were parked within yards of their home?

After commenting briefly on the house, our conversation soon turned almost instinctively to the question of whether we could ever make contact with them, particularly with Lilian. It would surely be unthinkable to disturb them in their advanced old age when the unwelcome incident of the inconvenient child had probably long since faded from their memories.

I sat there wondering about her. Grey and wizened now, no doubt, but I fondly imagined that she had once been blonde and blue eyed, rather like our daughter, Kate.

I had always thought that Kate had inherited her beauty from this unknown grandmother, but of course I had no evidence for that. People had said rather disconcertingly, "She doesn't look like either of you, does she?" Such observations may simply provoke amused smiles from those who are comfortably settled within their family, but to those who lack such security, they raise underlying uncertainties.

Unexpectedly, being in Andover that day brought back vague memories to Bev. I later discovered from his file that he had visited the town just ten days before his fifteenth birthday. He had never been there previously, and he did not know why he and Phyllis Savage were there then and he had long since forgotten the brief detour that took place on one of the most significant days of his life.

Chapter 5

So Near...

A 'son' and a 'brother' came home at last. It seemed so natural that no one thought to question why it had turned out this way.

It was August 4th 1955. That day happened to be Wilfred and Phyllis Savage's twenty-first wedding anniversary, but instead of celebrating together, Phyllis travelled alone by steam train from Eastleigh to London Waterloo station. She took underground trains across London to surface eventually at South Woodford station. Then she walked the mile and a half from the station to Mill Grove.

There Bev was waiting for her and, after brief farewells, Phyllis and Bev left together, he carrying a suitcase which contained all his belongings carefully prepared and packed by the staff.

It was a memorable day for them both because it was the day when he ceased to be a child in care and began his new life back in the home where he had been most loved and happy for the first five years of his childhood.

Wilfred and Phyllis's 'son', and Sheila's 'brother', came home at last. It seemed so right, so natural that no one thought to question why it had turned out this way.

A stressful meeting

Phyllis had two tasks to accomplish that day. Having completed the first, she and Bev travelled excitedly together from Waterloo station by steam train, not to Eastleigh, their final destination that evening, but to Andover, this small town some twenty-five miles to the north. She had something to do there before they could finally leave for home.

It was a very stressful day for the woman she met in a first floor solicitor's office. Phyllis Savage and Lilian Fletcher came face to face for the first time while Bev, completely unaware of what was happening upstairs, waited in the street below.

It was a painful meeting by all accounts, particularly for Lilian. Bev's file contained Phyllis's record of it in a letter written later to the director of Mill Grove at the time, Victor White.

"The day that we fetched Beverley everything went very well. I met Mrs Fletcher in the solicitor's room and I had to tell her how we came to have anything to do with Beverley. Mrs Froud had never told her that we looked after him for nearly five years. She was very distressed about it all. She told me Beverley's father promised to legally adopt him as soon as possible after his birth, she said she could see no other way out as she had a son four years old, she told me her husband forgave her and took her back, and she has a daughter 11 months younger than Beverley, she asked me for a photo of Beverley. ... I don't want him to know about it."

Phyllis asked her if she would like to see her son but she declined, requesting Phyllis to leave first with him so that they wouldn't meet.

Bev, of course, was unaffected by their meeting since he had no idea that his birth mother was so near but, when he later learned what had happened,

he only remembered a fairly transient sense of
disappointment. With all the changes ahead of
him as he settled into his new home and with the
world of work ahead, he was too preoccupied to be
concerned with a woman who had previously never
featured in his life.

When he read Phyllis's letter for the first time these
many years later his only comments were, "Well, she
asked for a photo', so I suppose that means she did
care … She could have thought to have given me a
photo' of herself."

A half-brother and sister
Subsequent visits to the Winchester Records Office
provided more insights into Lilian's family.

I discovered that she and Hector had, indeed, had
a son four years before Bev. Michael was born in
1936 and his birth was registered in Bristol. Bev had
speculated vaguely that his mother could have been
married already when he was born but somehow we
had never thought that she might have already given
birth to a child.

We had surmised that she had gone on to have
a family after Bev was born but it came as quite a
surprise to learn of a daughter born only eleven
months after him, a daughter who no doubt drew
Hector and Lilian together again and helped to close
the gap that threatened to ruin their relationship for
ever.

The records confirmed that June was born in
1941 and registered in Winchester. So Bev had a
half-brother and sister previously unknown to us.
I wondered where they might be living and if they
were aware of his existence. I thought not since such
indiscretions were not talked of openly at that time.

It was becoming obvious to us both that any
attempt on our part to track down Fletcher family

members would almost certainly cause distress to Hector and Lilian and, indeed, to their entire family. Their daughter would naturally want to know about the circumstances of her half-brother's birth and that could seriously jeopardise established family relationships so, with some reluctance, we dismissed the idea of ever making contact.

Who was responsible for his care?

Bev had long lived with the idea that his mother had simply given him up at birth and that she had just disappeared, but it seemed unlikely to me that Hector and Lilian would abandon him to the care of a single man in his thirties.

What would he do with a baby? He would surely not adopt and raise the child himself. He had no verifiable legal connection to the child and no DNA test was available to provide proof that he fathered the child. Ted had successfully escaped his responsibility for the child and was free to walk away since it was unlikely, I thought, that anyone would even know of his involvement except the Fletchers – and later the Frouds. Maybe it had always been in his mind that the Frouds would volunteer to care for Bev.

What Lilian knew

I assumed that Lilian was completely ignorant of what had happened to her baby until she met Phyllis in Andover but, putting together various pieces of information from letters in the file, it became clear that the Frouds had been in contact with her at the time application papers were sent to Mill Grove some five years previously.

Edwin Froud wrote to her when the search for a place for Bev was becoming desperate and the Fletchers' personal details appeared in papers submitted to the Home.

It must have come as a very unwelcome intrusion into their lives when Hector and Lilian suddenly received a letter demanding support for a child they had left in the care of his father ten years earlier. Edwin's letter to them was blunt and to the point, as he later explained:

> *"We have however made it plain to both parents of Beverley that they have to do something for him and to take the whole responsibility, but we will still give Beverley a home as long as we can or as long as he likes to stay."*

But no such support was forthcoming from either parent.

> *"From the onset the mother has not recognised the baby nor has she accepted any responsibility or contributed towards Beverley's maintenance."*

The Frouds had been left holding the baby – quite literally. It seems to have been entirely their choice at first but, with Daisy's rapidly declining health, it was becoming a nightmare from which they were understandably anxious to escape.

It was not entirely accurate to write of Lilian that she had thoughtlessly abandoned her responsibility for the child for, as I later gathered, it was the men, Ted and Hector, who agreed arrangements for the child's future. By all accounts Lilian was hardly consulted. Hector must have felt entirely justified ten years later in refusing to give support to another man's child. It seems most likely that he forbade Lilian to contribute anything, and who can blame him? He had generously legitimised his birth by giving him his name. Why would he give anything else?

Lilian did the best she could in the circumstances. She signed papers in the presence of a solicitor giving her consent for her son to be received into the children's home. There is no record of Hector also signing as the registered father of the child.

Chapter 6
BIG DADDY - LITTLE DADDY

E dward (Ted) Foderingham was born in Southampton on January 8th 1906 and died there of liver cancer eighty years later.

I discovered from the records that his mother, Kate, had died at the age of thirty-eight when he was just fifteen. His father, Edward Francis, was a quarter-master in the Merchant Navy and the Frouds understood that he had also died young leaving Ted without parents and a home so they took him in when he was in his early 'teens.

> "E.C. Foderingham came to live with us as a young lad roughly about twenty-six years ago as he lost his parents and as far as we knew had to leave his home and from then until he was called to the forces we kept him etc. looking more or less upon him as a son."

Big Daddy

In his prime he was an impressively tall, dark and attractive man who had a successful career in the insurance industry. Most people who met him seemed to like him although he had a reputation for loving the company of women whom he openly flattered and obviously impressed.

Beverley's father practically ignores him... and we have heard that he has denied him.

He developed expensive tastes and appeared to have more money than an insurance agent could earn at that time, owning and running a car long before it was common for working people to enjoy such luxury. He married Marjorie Badham in Llanelli, West Wales, in 1943 and they had three children, Stephen, Patricia and Vivian, all educated in fee-paying schools.

But some found to their cost that Ted was not to be trusted. The Frouds, for example, opened their home to him and his growing family and supported him over many years but, as Edwin Froud revealed in a letter he wrote to Mill Grove, he took advantage even of these his most generous benefactors.

> "We were told Beverley was the son of a relative, a brother we think, and that Edward Foderingham would be responsible for him. We felt sorry for the baby who of course had no one and for 10 months he was in a nursing home and as far as we can remember we paid the costs or most of them.
>
> "When the baby came from the nursing home which was just about the time the war started, he was put out to nurse and for the five years we paid all expenses. All this being done in the hope and inference that ECF would be fully responsible for this baby as promised, but we did not know at that time that he was the father of it.
>
> "The time came when the father was demobbed and one of the first things to be done was to have Beverley home.
>
> "In due course we learnt that he was the father of Beverley ... Beverley's father practically ignores him, although they are living in our home, he does not offer to pay one penny for his keep and we have heard that he has denied Beverley."

Ted's predicament was not, of course, uncommon during and after the war and, if he had been a 'thirties something' single man living today, he would not have been considered particularly promiscuous. His marriage to Marjorie lasted over forty years and, as far as we know, he proved to be a responsible and loving parent to his other three children.

However, there is no denying that he neglected his firstborn son and presumed upon the good-will of his long-suffering friends the Frouds, who may have been happy to have had it so had it not been for Daisy's unexpected and rather rapid decline. In the event they became bitterly resentful of the way they had been treated as Daisy explained in a letter written to Herbert White in December 1950.

> "When EC Foderingham was demobbed he came home again and took up the threads of looking after Beverley with this difference, he did not contribute towards the expense. Later we found out that he was married two years before.
>
> "Consequent upon all this happening we naturally wanted to know about Beverley's future, for as you can see all our sympathy, generosity and care for Beverley was thrown back at us and in fact we were left with the baby.
>
> "...This is briefly the whole story, excepting that EC Foderingham, and his whole family are still living with us - again a flagrant case where generosity and kindness has been abused, but the father of Beverley does not take any notice of Beverley, does not contribute anything towards his keep, and very, very little towards his clothing etc. and upon this may I be excused if I do not make any further observations, but leave this to your own experience and imagination. W. D. Froud (Mrs.)"

Little Daddy

Edwin Froud, a short, balding, hard working man

in his late fifties, was devoted to his wife, Daisy.
He did his best to care for the young boy whom
she had brought into their lives but, as she became
increasingly unwell, she demanded more of his
attention and the boy became a burden he could well
have done without. Bev remembers him as a sighing,
weary man and this image is confirmed by an
observer of the family who commented, "He always
seemed to me to be a rather sad man, rather put
upon." His life must have become almost unbearable
at times.

His day began early with clearing up after the six
cats that Daisy insisted were kept in at night and
who were not well house-trained. Then he would
leave to go to his work as a clerk in the office of an
engineering company in Southampton only to return
in the evening to wait on Daisy, do more housework
and try to contain the frustrated child who also
demanded his attention.

Edwin was the only one in the household who
seemed to give any practical care to Bev. He was
the one who took him out of the house as often as
he could to give Daisy a break and to allow him to
release his pent-up energy. He once set up a little
wireless for Bev to listen to in another room when he
was ill.

That was the only occasion that Bev can remember
sleeping in his own bedroom. It seems likely that one
of the other children had to be moved out to make
it possible. He mostly remembers sleeping between
Daisy and Edwin, or at least in their room. Bev called
him 'Little Daddy' and Ted he called 'Big Daddy' or
'Airman Daddy', a title that must have fed Marjorie's
resentment every time she heard it.

Sunday school
Like many children in the post-war years, Bev was
sent to a Sunday school which was held in the

small front room of the home of a widow woman, Mrs Tucker. She, with her friends, Mr and Mrs Bell, were concerned that there was no provision for the spiritual education of children living in their immediate area of Chandlers Ford so she opened her home. Hearing of the class, Edwin and Daisy were only too pleased to send Bev along so as to have precious time to themselves.

These many years later he still remembers some of the Bible stories he was taught then and, such was the influence of the Sunday School teachers on him, that he unexpectedly began to take an interest in the Bible, unexpected because he was not the kind of child who easily settled to quiet activities of any kind and especially not to reading. However, he recalls having a Bible and reading Psalm 1 while confined to bed alongside Daisy Froud – but as far as he can recall he didn't get as far as Psalm 2.

SOMEBODY'S SON

Chapter 7

CHINA DOLL

The garden of the bungalow in which the Frouds lived in Chandlers Ford had a long frontage onto Leigh Road with tall pine trees overarching the entrance which dropped their needles and carpeted the drive. A separate garage had adjoining rooms and contained an ancient dusty open-topped car with a high leather-back seat and big headlamps. Occasionally Bev would escape from the confines of the bedroom, sneak into the garage and sit in the grand front seat and play with the controls. We imagine that the vehicle was left in store there by the owner of the property since it had not left the garage for a very long time.

Behind the bungalow was an extensive south facing garden, mainly laid to lawn, with tall hedges running down either side of it. An orchard backed onto a small prisoner-of-war camp at its southern boundary and Bev remembers the alarm created in the household when a man was seen moving through the undergrowth in the orchard. A gardener would appear now and again but he made little impression on the large expanse of land – and Phyllis Savage came to clean for the family.

SOMEBODY'S SON

Daisy Froud

Daisy Froud was a complex character who ruled her domain and her servants. A proud and capable woman, Mum Savage described her as a 'china doll', slim, smart and demanding. She had once been very attractive and, even when she became unwell, she continued to enjoy her expensive clothes, fur coats and wraps. A large, framed studio photograph of her hung above the fireplace in the central lounge of the bungalow, showing her in the full flush of youth and sporting the distinctive bobbed hairstyle of the day.

There was money in the Froud family. Where it came from remains a mystery; where it went has gradually come to light as I have gathered more information. Some of it clearly paid for the baby's care first in the nursing home and then with the Savages.

Daisy enjoyed buying Bev expensive white romper suits when he was a toddler, an altogether impractical choice for such an active boy, and as he grew older she dressed him in tweed with knickerbockers and cap. Mum Savage described him as sometimes looking like "Little Lord Fauntleroy".

Sheila was six years old when he first arrived in her home. She accepted him as one of the family without question, it seems, and found herself rescuing his cap on more than one occasion when he was teased by other children in the village. Studio photographs taken during those early years confirm that the white-blond haired child was immaculately dressed.

Later he was also bought expensive presents, like the magnificent rocking horse that he found beside the bed one Christmas morning and the new bicycle that he was allowed to ride on the lawn for a few days before it was strung up in the garage, tantalisingly out of reach, unused because there was no one to go out with him and teach him to ride it.

In one of his letters Edwin Froud describes his wife as being devoted to Bev. After her death he wrote to Herbert White:

"I also want to say how glad I am that the Lord has placed Beverley in your care and in that respect I have only one regret that is that my wife was not able to see the effects of her long endeavours. How glad she would have been to have seen him and the others so well and happy.

> **They found themselves increasingly confined to one bedroom in the bungalow.**

... I do hope that Beverley will be a good boy and proceed to advance, for he is alone and we tried so much to plan his future but outside circumstances prevented this. Although he is not naturally ours, my dear wife counted him as such and her love was lavished upon him, and God willing I will carry on her self-imposed task, in the great hope that Beverley in the future will be a worthy memorial to her."

But Bev has no recollection of any real affection from Daisy Froud. She certainly did her best to train him to be presentable in polite society but she became so unwell that it was as much as she could do to simply contain the hyperactive child. She was fifty years of age when she took responsibility for him. She had no children of her own and no first-hand experience of caring for a child. In the event it all proved to be too much for her.

Her health finally broke down in the summer of 1949 when she had a stroke, leaving her face partially paralysed, a tragedy for someone who had been so proud of her appearance. She and Edwin, with the boy, found themselves increasingly confined to one bedroom in the bungalow.

When he came home from school Bev would spend his time there, lying on the bed with Daisy until Edwin arrived home from work around six o'clock. His overriding memory of those years is of being unbearably confined. His later quite severe claustrophobia may well hark back to those early experiences. Another legacy from that time is that he is not at all keen to have animals in the house.

Lost luxuries
Although his entrance into the children's home changed his life entirely and brought him lasting benefit, he did leave behind him an experience of

an affluent home where he had begun to learn the habits and opinions of the middle-classes at a time of grinding post-war austerity.

There may have been few children who entered Mill Grove at that time with a similar background to his although dysfunctional families and children in need are to be found in every strata of society.

It was common for children in the home to feel that they shouldn't be in care and to tell stories of their rich parents who would soon come to take them away. Bev had as much reason to dream that dream as any and to feel keenly the loss of his former material advantages.

One or two have conjectured that his mixed feelings when he returns to Mill Grove arise from the fact that, since he has had what some might call a 'successful' life, he subconsciously wishes to distance himself from his years in care. I doubt that is the case since he has continued to maintain contact with the home throughout his life – and I know that he doesn't view himself as especially successful, rather the reverse.

A more likely explanation is that as a ten year old he left behind him a materially privileged existence when he entered Mill Grove and the contrast between the two exaggerated his sense of loss and deprivation and made him feel even more that he should never have gone into care and that he didn't fit in.

|| It was
not long
before the
two women
began to
fight

Chapter 8

SECRETS

Marjorie Foderingham, Ted's wife, was a young, petite attractive blonde when she came to the bungalow – and another dominant personality. It was not long before the two women began to fight and it seems likely that the stress caused by their mutual animosity was, at least in part, responsible for Daisy's stroke and rapid decline in health.

To be fair to her, two years after her marriage to Ted, Marjorie found herself in an impossible situation - a twenty one year old pregnant wife, far from home, sharing a house with a woman whom she quickly came to hate, and with another woman's child who was a constant reminder of her husband's promiscuity. It is little wonder that Edwin Froud wrote of her:

> *"... added to all this is the antagonism of Beverley's father's wife who is by no means womanly or humane in any sense of the words."*

Ted and Marjorie went on to have two more children over the next few years.

> She was far too inquisitive and persistent to be fobbed off with lies

A puzzle

Why Ted took her to the bungalow, and why Edwin and Daisy agreed to have them there, is puzzling. Marjorie herself may well have been entirely ignorant of what awaited her and shocked when she discovered that the child who also moved in around the time she arrived was Ted's.

If Ted and Daisy thought that they could keep Bev's identity secret from Marjorie, they were much mistaken. He clearly had his father's features and skin colouring and Marjorie proved far too inquisitive and persistent to be fobbed off with lies.

So, since Ted knew full well the situation into which he was taking his wife and mother-to-be, could he not have anticipated that the arrangement was doomed to failure from the outset? Why would he knowingly take her into such a dire situation?

Daisy was fifteen years older than their young lodger and, although Edwin described him as being like a son to them, that description did not tell the full story of their relationship. It seems likely that, unknown to him, Daisy and Ted had been much closer than that.

Letters and money

Phyllis was present when, following Daisy's death, Edwin discovered letters among her possessions that appear to have passed between her and Ted.

I asked them about the letters. "Were they affectionate letters as between a mother figure and a son?" "Oh no!" they replied, "Definitely not. For a start, you don't usually write 'My darling Teddy' to your lodger, or even to your son for that matter, do you?" They said little more about what they had learned but their reticence conveyed the impression that the relationship had gone much further than a purely maternal one.

There was no denying that the letters were written by Daisy, as Edwin confirmed, but why had she kept them among her things only for them to be discovered after her death? Did her illness simply overtake her or was it, perhaps, her way of confessing her affection for Ted to Edwin? Perhaps it was all just a fantasy on her part? Were the letters ever sent? Where were the reciprocal letters from him? If there had been any, she would surely have kept them, wouldn't she?

Whatever the truth, Daisy undoubtedly had a hold over Ted and was possessive of him. From his point of view she was a passport to inexpensive, if not free lodgings for him and his growing family – and more beside.

Edwin was visibly shocked and distressed after Daisy's death to find that every bank account that he turned to had been emptied. When he died in 1954 his estate was worth less than £900 even after the sale of a business that he and Daisy had owned together. So it seems that Daisy and Ted were bound by secrets that even those closest to them would only discover when it was impossible to address them.

I gathered that Daisy may have known all along that Bev was Ted's son and had agreed to take some responsibility for him without consulting Edwin. In so doing she bound Ted to her and, since she was also supplying him with money, it is no wonder that he returned to live with her.

So, from 1945 until 1951 Bev was living with two women, neither of whom were his mother and both of whom used him as a pawn in a game to gain control and undermine each other. It was by no means the cosy, well-mannered, middle-class, affluent household that it may have appeared to onlookers.

In 1940 there had been just a middle aged couple

> It was by no means the cosy, well-mannered, middle-class, affluent household that it may have appeared to onlookers

and their lodger living in that bungalow. Nine years later it contained four warring adults and four children all under ten years of age. Daisy, experienced in controlling and manipulating situations to suit herself, met her match in Marjorie.

It was a pitifully dysfunctional household – and secrets known only to Ted and Daisy made the situation even more tense and threatening than it first appeared.

Chapter 9
RUNNING WILD

B ev was registered in schools in Chandlers Ford and Eastleigh but he was a sickly child who was often too unwell to attend, so he fell behind in his education. Although his identity card and ration book were registered in the name of Fletcher, he was known at school by the surname Froud, the schools seeming to accept that Edwin and Daisy were his official guardians.

Deprivation
As an adult Bev was mildly surprised one day to be asked by a close friend to speak on 'Deprivation and its Effects'. He, like most children, accepted the circumstances of his early years as 'normal' and, even as an adult, had not thought of himself as particularly deprived.

In many ways he was not. Other children fared much worse than he and Mill Grove contained many whose poverty and deprivation had been extreme. There are well documented accounts of children who suffered greatly as a result of WW2 and who remained ignorant of the fact that close family members were still alive when they were shipped out to help populate Australia, Canada

His deprivation was more subtle but no less real

and Rhodesia. Many who still live carry with them memories of abuse from those who were charged with their care and protection. Most never saw their parents or siblings again although some have returned to Britain in their later years to be reunited with their remaining relatives.

By comparison Bev was physically very well provided for. His deprivation was more subtle but no less real.

Raised in a home with three other young children, he was excluded from their company. They had the run of the house while he was contained, often feeling disgraced and responsible for the troubles of the household. He received little straightforward, unconditional affection. The adults around him claimed authority over him but argued incessantly about who was responsible for him. He belonged only to one of them, his father, who never owned him as his child.

He had no one who had the time or inclination to listen to him or care enough to control him for his own sake. In the end he became an embarrassment for them all, trapped as they were each with their insuperable problems and their dreams of freedom.

A private fantasy world

Despite everything, Bev did not present as an intimidated, browbeaten child. Rather he retreated into his private fantasy world free of adults, a world of plans and adventures.

He somehow got that bike down from the rafters in the garage and rode it to school one day, despite the fact that he couldn't balance properly and the tyres were flat. Child-like though, he had not thought his action through and it was only as he got near to the school gate that it dawned on him that he would be found with the bike, so he hid it under a near-

SOMEBODY'S SON

by river bridge. Its absence was soon noticed back
at Leigh Road and a telephone call to the school
ensured that he was in trouble - again.

His many misdemeanours must have caused the
adults considerable anxiety and frustration, like the
morning he ran out from behind the school bus to be
hit by a car; that brought the police to their door, and
the huge cut he sustained on his forehead when he
ran into the school gate; that scar remains to this day
among other permanent memorials to his youthful
wildness.

More daring adventures
As he grew a little older and changed school, he
gained confidence and became more adventurous,
sometimes deliberately missing the bus home.

Typically, he had planned the almost two mile route
from Shakespeare Road School through an alley-
way, over the railway bridge and across the park to
the shops in Eastleigh town centre. There he would
while away an hour window shopping until he felt it
was time to make his way back to the bungalow.

He had worked out where to get the bus to
Chandlers Ford and on the journey he constructed
excuses for his late appearance - 'The bus went
without me'- 'They didn't wait for me' - 'Someone
stole my bus money'. Whatever the displeasure of
the frantic adults who vented their fury on him when
he arrived, a couple of hours of freedom were worth
it all.

Stealing
It was just a short step from looking in shop
windows to setting his heart on things he wanted.

Having found ways to escape adult attention for a
while, he now needed to fund his adventures so he
searched out sources of finance. At one time he took

> It was a rare face-to-face encounter with his father and he remembers that look still.

as much as seven shillings from Daisy's purse, only equivalent to thirty five pence today, but a significant sum of money then. With that he bought himself an articulated toy lorry, but once again he hadn't thought his action through and when he arrived back at the bungalow he realised he couldn't take it in without being questioned, so he dug a hole and buried it in the front garden. Unfortunately for him, Marjorie was watching from the kitchen window and quickly marched out to uncover the evidence and ensure that he was thoroughly interrogated and reprimanded.

Was this the occasion or another when he was arraigned before 'Airman Daddy' as he was eating his evening meal in the lounge? Ted looked at him as his crimes were recounted and demands made that something be done about the troublesome boy. It was a rare face-to-face encounter with his father and he remembers that look still, a look of annoyance – and of helplessness. Nothing came of it.

The champion

Wilfred, Phyllis and Sheila had come to regard Bev as one of the family and he was to find in Phyllis a fierce and loyal champion.

She was not an openly affectionate 'mother figure', but she would have done anything to defend the child whom she had come to love as her own. Shiela remembers that it was to her father, Wilfred, that she would turn for cuddles and he was the one who read her stories and sang to her although Phyllis's love for her and for Bev was beyond question.

She somehow arranged to be employed as a cleaner in the bungalow in Chandlers Ford only because she saw it as a way to keep an eye on what was happening to him. It was not long before she grew indignant at what she saw and heard and, true

to form, she gave 'Foddy' "a piece of my mind".
The family knew exactly what she meant by that
phrase and wondered if her employment would be
terminated immediately, but nothing much changed
until Daisy's deteriorating health made the situation
intolerable for the occupants of the bungalow.

At that point Phyllis heard talk of putting the boy
into a boarding school or home and she seized the
opportunity to play a part in helping to secure a
place for him if she could. The events of the next
months, and her part in them, proved to be vital
in turning his life around and pointing him in a
completely different direction.

SOMEBODY'S SON

Chapter 10
THE CARER

Coincidences are a common experience of life for everyone, of course, but for those who have a living faith in a personal God who cares for his children, they often take on a significance far beyond chance happenings with no particular meaning. Profound outcomes often hang on the slimmest of providential threads as was the case in Bev's life.

Consider, for example, the way in which the Savages came to care for him. What brought them together?

Daisy no doubt considered carefully her choice of carers for the child but she could have no idea of just how important her decision would be. She saw his placement with the Savages as a temporary arrangement with employees who she did not consider sufficiently important to mention in any subsequent correspondence. From among hundreds of ordinary working class families living simply in modest houses in a Hampshire village, Daisy unwittingly chose parents for Bev and end-of-life care for herself and her husband.

So what persuaded her to choose Wilfred and Phyllis Savage to care for the boy and what made them respond so generously in opening their home not only to him, but later to Daisy and Edwin too?

Phyllis's expectations

Phyllis was born in Newport, Isle of Wight, in August 1912, the firstborn of Ernest and Emily Munt. Six years later Lilian joined her sister but the family suffered a heavy blow when, as a baby, Lily developed infantile paralysis, now known as polio, and was left with a semi-paralysed leg. She wore a calliper all her life and needed a wheelchair. So from early on in her life Phyllis cared for her sister and this became such a way of life for her that it seemed to shape her expectations of what her future would be.

Phyllis and Lily's parents were quiet, serious people and when they moved to Melbourne Street in Newport, they began to attend a little independent chapel where Ernest helped in the Sunday school. There the sisters were taught the Christian faith but Phyllis never expressed any personal belief herself.

As with many young girls of working class families at the time, she went into service at the age of fourteen and was employed to do fairly menial work in grand houses. She had several posts in the next four or five years, her habit of speaking her mind rather directly may well have accounted for her moving on fairly frequently.

She began a friendship with a young man named Les, but such was the strength of her father's disapproval of him, that he made arrangements for her to leave the Island and take up a position on the mainland where relatives were asked to keep an eye on her. Phyllis bitterly resented her father's intervention and the relationship between them became strained.

The relatives in question were Ernest's brother, Bill, and his wife, Floss, who lived in Bishopstoke. Floss was Wilfred Savage's older sister, so the Savages and the Munts were already related before Phyllis arrived on the scene. She spent much of her free time at her Uncle Bill's and Aunty Floss's home and it was there that she first met her future husband, Wilfred. He was seventeen years her senior.

For all her rebellious nature and plain speaking, Phyllis was like her mother in that she was a serious young woman prone to anxiety and depression. Wilfred, on the other hand, came from a family of entertainers. Jim, his brother, and Wilf himself had earned a reputation in the village for their showmanship and their sister, Floss, was also happily eccentric.

Wilfred

Wilfred was rather like an overgrown, mischievous schoolboy, with a childlike sense of humour. Sheila called him 'an old rogue', lovable, of course.

Stories of his many adventures abound like the time when he thrust his garden fork into some hard soil only to pin his wellington boot to the ground with a prong going straight through it. He gingerly removed the fork and hobbled the half-mile home to call out for Phyllis's help as he entered the house. She removed the boot expecting blood to pour from it only to find that the prong had gone between his toes and, apart from a slight graze, there was nothing to show for the incident.

He had a strong, pleasant baritone voice and sang throughout his life starting in St Mary's church choir as a boy soloist. He would proudly relate the story of his performance in Winchester Cathedral under the baton of Sir Malcolm Sargent. In later years he could be heard amusing the village drinkers in The Anglers Inn and The Anchor pub down by the river where his singing was legendary. He worked hard by day as a pipe fitter in the steam locomotive works, a physically demanding job, but when the evenings came he was known to dress rather fashionably and enjoy himself.

In later years all the grandchildren just loved him, ours included. They called him 'Grandad Cuckoo' because, when he could think of nothing else, he made the bird sound to entertain them. His aversion to doctors and dentists meant that he was left in his later years with virtually no teeth and a somewhat battered body but despite this neglect he lived until he was ninety eight years of age and never lost his sense of humour.

Some months after his death Philip, our eldest son, wrote, "I still miss Grandad. The family just isn't the same without him." That was true. We all missed this funny, loveable, sometimes exasperating elder member of the family.

Quite what attracted the rather sober young Phyllis to him was a mystery at first. When he teased her, which he often did, she would almost invariably rise to the bait, exasperated by his nonsense. He embarrassed her, indeed all of us, at times and she would famously give him one of her looks which left no one in any doubt about what she was thinking.

He was a man of the world, much older than she, so it came as no surprise that her father objected once again to her plan to marry Wilfred. But this time Phyllis was on the mainland out of his reach and in

ll Love came
later.

no mood to listen. She was determined to escape the religious strictures of her parents and to break free from working as a maid in someone else's home if she could. She had the opportunity to begin a family of her own in a new house that Wilfred would build for them in the village. She wasn't looking for a 'father figure' to marry, as might be conjectured. Actually, she became a mother figure to him and assumed her familiar role as a carer once again.

But there was another reason for her marriage to Wilfred. After he had died she rather surprised me one day when she revealed, "I didn't really marry Dad for love you know. When his mother was very ill I promised her that I would look after him. Love came later." And she revealed one more detail in a conversation with Sheila, her daughter, when she confessed, "I felt sorry for him."

It didn't altogether surprise us that she entered marriage that way because it was so characteristic of Phyllis to commit herself to caring when she came across a need. It was a role that she occupied throughout her entire life. She just couldn't help herself.

Marriage and family

Phyllis and Wilf married on August 4th 1934 and, after a few months of living with Auntie Floss, were able to move just opposite into their modest, brand new detached house with its large garden. Nine months later Sheila was born.

Phyllis's reasons for marrying may not have been the most romantic yet their marriage lasted for well over fifty years. She was faithful to her promise to care for him, which she did well into her 80's when she was no longer able to manage him at home and he went into care.

As a young mother at home with her baby

daughter, she continued to do what she had always done, take on anyone she happened to meet who needed her care. She kept an open home and was always off doing someone's shopping or cleaning their home. I asked Sheila how Phyllis had come to be friendly with Ted Foderingham and the Frouds and she replied, "Oh, you know Mum. She would take anyone in."

'Foddy' was known to be in the habit of accepting hospitality from his clients and such was his friendly disposition and readiness to chat that even the indomitable Auntie Floss was charmed by him and used to have him in for tea and home-made cake.

Once, when Lily was visiting from the Isle of Wight, she remembers being flattered by him as he admired her hands and long fingers. So the Savages and the Munts were familiar to Ted and maybe it was he who recommended them to Daisy as suitable people to be approached to care for the baby. Whatever the prompting, Daisy's choice of the Savages proved to be inspired.

SOMEBODY'S SON

Chapter 11
LOVE BEYOND DOUBT

At the time that Phyllis was approached about caring for Bev she had experienced what she later called a 'phantom pregnancy' that left her suffering from some kind of nervous debility. Apparently Daisy, on hearing of her condition, had concluded that it might help her if she actually had a living child to care for.

Memories and impressions

The arrangement with the Savages was to be temporary. At six years of age Sheila remembers the baby being brought into the house in Scotter Road carried in a blue carry cot. It is likely that Bev was between nine and ten months old at that time so rather large for a carry cot one might think. However, he had been suffering a great deal with sickness and diarrhoea while in the nursing home and there was some possibility of losing him, so maybe his condition required that he travel lying down. He continued to be very unwell during his first months with the Savages and remained susceptible to sickness into adult life. If the family planned to take him out on a train or on the ferry to the Isle of Wight they learned from experience not

Just like a boy!

to tell him beforehand since the anticipation would invariably result in him being too ill to go.

There were many disturbed nights at that time as the port of Southampton became a target for German bombing and, each time the siren went and he was grabbed from his bed to be taken to the Anderson shelter in the garden or the communal air raid shelter in the street outside, he would be sick.

Sheila also remembered his rocking. Before he went to sleep he would get onto his knees in his cot and rock from side to side. Sometimes he did this so violently that the cot moved across the room. The sound could be heard throughout the house.

Whether caring for Bev helped Phyllis with her nervous problems is doubtful, though it probably meant she was too busy to think much about herself.

Almost everyone who has any memories of the young boy speak of him as boisterous, having a loud voice and being a bit of a rascal. He would cause a certain amount of havoc wherever he went, rushing at life with a great deal of enthusiasm.

Such children are demanding, requiring constant attention and are hard to control, but they can also be very endearing. "Just like a boy!" one lady remarked as she described how he was asked to sweep up after a Harvest Festival display had been dismantled only to scatter debris in all directions. Another recalls, "The earliest memory I have of Beverley was when he was about three years old. We went somewhere on a coach and Phyllis had this little boy with her. He was wearing a bright red beret", a fashion accessory from the Frouds, no doubt.

Payment
Ted Foderingham and the Frouds visited the Savages from time to time during the war years. Sheila remembers Ted arriving in his Air Force uniform,

bringing her presents and paying her parents for the child's care.

Bev was somewhat taken aback when I mentioned one day that money had changed hands to pay for his keep. For some reason he had never considered that possibility and found it unpleasant to hear that Phyllis was paid to look after him. A moment's thought, however, was enough to convince him that it had to be so, but the idea that they might only have agreed to take care of him because they were paid, somehow made the relationship seem more like a business transaction than unconditional love.

It is something that must occur to thousands of children who are in short-term foster homes with many different carers.

Abrupt separation

Then, one day the Frouds arrived and left with Bev to return to Chandlers Ford. The parting was abrupt and the family was left wounded.

Having come to regard him as one of their own, all they could hope for now was to have him visit and stay with them from time to time when the Frouds agreed to it. The pain of the separation was illustrated by an event that was spoken of in the family for many years afterwards.

One lunch time, as Wilf was walking through Eastleigh returning to work for his afternoon shift at the Railway Works, the young boy saw him from across the road. He broke free from Edwin, dashed somewhat recklessly between the traffic on the busy main road to throw his arms around his Uncle Wilf, dressed as he was in his flat cap, dirty overalls and oily boots. At last they reluctantly let each other go and Wilf, an emotional man at the best of times, went on his way to work, supported by his friends, weeping like a child.

> Wilf went on his way to work, supported by his friends, weeping like a child.

There was never any doubt about the love that the Savages had for him. They gave as generously to him as they did to Sheila, their own daughter. In fact, they made considerable sacrifices to help him especially through the three years of his theological training when we were in need.

Exceptional generosity

Wilf continued to work after the statutory retirement age and he and Phyllis remained in their house rather than move into something more suitable in their old age so that they could leave the property for Sheila and Bev to sell and share the proceeds.

For us it meant that, having lived in church property until we were fifty years old, we were at last able to make a deposit on our first home using the proceeds from the sale. Wilfred and Phyllis were a far from wealthy couple, but they enriched us in every way.

Chapter 12
CARAVAN MISSION

B ishopstoke sprawls across the south side of a gently climbing hill. At its feet, to the south and west of the village, lie the meadows through which meanders the river Itchen on its way from Winchester to the English Channel.

The residents of the village are served by two churches. St. Mary's, the Anglican Church with its bell tower and surrounding cemetery, was built at the turn of the 20th century to replace an earlier building lower down in the village by the river. It now sits at the top of the village, or upper 'Stoke as it is known, an area generally regarded as a somewhat more desirable part of the village in which to live.

The Savages had their home in lower 'Stoke where the Methodist Chapel was located in Spring Lane opposite the river and near to the few shops that served the area. The chapel was an unprepossessing tin hut but the people who attended it were devout and active in the village.

It was not long before Phyllis came to know them and to send Sheila and Bev to the Methodist Sunday school. Her father and mother had never given up hope that their daughter might one day return to the faith they held dear, so when an opportunity

When the roll is called up yonder I'll be there.

arose for them to rekindle her interest, they took full advantage of it.

An invitation that changed lives

There were at that time travelling evangelists who moved from village to village teaching children and preaching the good news concerning Jesus Christ to their parents and friends. They were known as Missioners and the organisation which sponsored them gloried in the title of 'The Caravan Mission to Village Children'.

The Missioner for Hampshire was a charming, warm-hearted, white haired man named Joe Bush. He towed his caravan around the villages and set up his marquee in the fields of friendly farmers or on village greens.

It just so happened that during a mission that he conducted in Newport on the Isle of Wight, he met Ernest Munt, Phyllis's father. On hearing that his next mission was to be held in Bishopstoke, Ernest requested Joe to call on his daughter and encourage her to attend the meetings, and this he did.

In later years Phyllis recalled how she opened the door to him and knew straightaway who he was, why he was there and who had sent him. But instead of resenting her father's intrusion as previously, she agreed to attend the mission meetings with a neighbour, a change of attitude no doubt influenced by her new-found Methodist friends and also by the fact that five year old Beverley had only recently been taken from the family and they were in distress.

Each day first children and then adults would meet in the open or in the marquee to sing hymns and choruses and to hear the Bible explained by Joe and it was at one of those meetings that Phyllis was very challenged, not so much by the preacher, but by a familiar old hymn which was a favourite at that time,

"When the roll is called up yonder I'll be there." She had no certainty that her name was listed among believers in the Lord Jesus Christ who would be safe on judgement day, so she prayed that evening asking God for forgiveness for her neglect of him and she placed her faith in the Lord Jesus Christ as the One who would save her and take her at last to be with Him. So she became a Christian. Sheila, ten years old, also committed her life to Jesus Christ at this time.

This simple experience changed Phyllis's entire outlook on life and gave greater focus to her already generous care of other people. But it soon posed problems within her marriage since Wilfred's instinctive reaction to the news of her conversion was to be even more mischievous and contrary than before, causing her to give him plenty of those famous looks of disapproval. However, despite many personal difficulties Phyllis grew in her Christian faith encouraged by her friends at the Methodist Chapel.

A new church

But the congregation was growing restless. Within Methodism there was seldom one regular preacher in the pulpits of smaller chapels. Different ministers and laymen were appointed to lead services and preach each week around a circuit of churches.

Some respected Bible teachers visited the Bishopstoke congregation periodically but for the most part preachers were less able and their preaching was often little more than a 'few blessed thoughts'. This disappointed and frustrated those who were keen to understand the Bible's teaching more thoroughly.

Finally, on January 23rd 1946, seventeen members of the congregation met in a private home in the village to consider what to do about the situation.

A vital link in the chain of events that led to Bev's entrance into Mill Grove.

They reluctantly agreed to form a new church and held their first public meeting the following Sunday in the village school where many of them, and their parents before them, had been educated. Phyllis's name appears among the members who formed Bishopstoke Evangelical Church.

Feeling vulnerable and isolated, it was not long after its formation that it joined the FIEC. No one could have possibly guessed at that time that the lively, mischievous boy who appeared among them from time to time would in the future become a leader of that Fellowship.

A Divine 'coincidence'

The Harris family had five children all of whom were taken to the church by their parents. When the time came for her to leave school, Dorothy, one of their daughters, decided that she would like to work with children and somehow, no-one now remembers how, she heard of a Christian Children's Home that had branches in Woodford and in Tiptree, Essex, 150 miles away. She applied to the Home and was accepted as a staff member assigned to work in Tiptree where she became known as 'Sister' Dorothy, a title common to all female staff at the time.

She was rather young to be working so far away from home so it was no surprise that she remained there for only a comparatively short period, but her adventure into child care proved to be a vital link in the chain of events that led to Bev's entrance into Mill Grove.

Chapter 13
ENDS AND BEGINNINGS

The church in Bishopstoke naturally took an interest in the work to which one of its young people had gone and as news of the Home began to filter through, Phyllis decided that she would suggest to the Frouds that they might consider Mill Grove as a suitable place for Bev.

Negotiations with Mill Grove
They took up her suggestion and began corresponding with Herbert White who, after a brief delay, dispatched an application form to them. A letter of acknowledgement from Daisy reads:

> *"The question of Beverley being placed under your care is having my serious and careful consideration."*

Whether other options were considered as seriously is not altogether clear although I discovered later that Lilian Fletcher was also trying to find a suitable boarding school for him.

However, the unresolved question of who would pay the fees frustrated the process and brought enquiries to an abrupt end since no one was willing to accept that it was their responsibility. One of the early queries that Daisy raised was, *"What sum would be required per week that is on a general average?"* The reply came back, *"Ten shillings per week would help."*

There was some delay in returning the application form as Daisy explained, *"I am not yet able to send the Form as I have to obtain signatures of both parents."* Lilian was contacted and she signed, but for Ted, appending his name to it posed a serious problem and this is what caused the delay.

Ted's signature on a form accompanied by the boy's birth certificate that named Lilian and Hector Fletcher as the parents would look distinctly odd and would require an explanation. It could be regarded as his admission of responsibility for the child - and he wasn't about to agree to that. And anyway, the boy was called Froud at the time so, since they had assumed responsibility for him, why wouldn't they sign the application form?

In the event the form was completed and eventually sent off on November 6th 1950, signed indeed by Edwin Froud as the applicant and witnessed by Phyllis. I could find no form in his file with the signatures of Ted and Lilian although they were both named as the boy's father and mother.

Edwin wrote a letter to accompany the form in which he said:

"May I ask, can Beverley's name be kept under mine, Froud, we do not mind this, in fact we would rather have it that way, for we have the boy's future at heart. The birth certificate can be obtained and sent forward if desired."

As might be expected, Herbert White insisted on clarifying the situation and asked for a copy of the birth certificate. Having received it, he wrote again asking for an explanation as to why the father's name was given as Hector Fletcher on the certificate and Edward Foderingham on the form.

We are keen to help this sad case

If Edwin and Daisy had hoped to get through the process without revealing too much, they were to be disappointed. Daisy wrote in reply:

> "I note your queries, and really I had expected to have them, but I thought I would go as far as I could in this matter, in the way we should like it to go if possible."

Herbert White would have none of it and on January 24th 1951 he wrote again:

> "Thank you for your full letter. One last point comes to mind which we would like you to clear up. Seeing that Beverley Fletcher is entered on the birth certificate and Mr and Mrs Fletcher are entered as his father and mother (presumably accepting responsibility for the boy) why are they not supporting the child, as it would appear they should do? Kindly reply as soon as possible - we are keen to help this sad case."

Edwin replied on his wife's behalf:

> "I note your queries, and to the best of my ability I will try to explain all that which you want to know. It is a difficult problem to explain by letter - it would have been so much better could we come to see you, but unfortunately Mrs Froud is unable to travel."

The letter went on to cover much the same ground as the one sent by his wife in the previous December. The only direct answer to Mr White's query concerning the Fletchers supporting the child was, "In due course we learnt that he (ECF) was the father of Beverley and who the mother is, but from the onset the mother has not recognised the baby nor has she *accepted responsibility or contributed towards Beverley's maintenance."*

Moving in with the Savages

Early in 1951, with Daisy's declining health, Phyllis suggested that she, Edwin and Bev move to their home in Bishopstoke so that she could care for Daisy. This couldn't have been easy for any of them.

The Savage's compact three bedroom detached house had just one bathroom upstairs and an outside toilet. Fitting four adults, Sheila their fifteen year old daughter and ten year old Bev into that home presented a huge challenge, but they were determined to do it. Phyllis lit a fire in the small grate in the best front bedroom to keep them all comfortable and to make them feel at home as they settled in.

In his anxiety to keep Bev from becoming a nuisance to their hosts, Edwin became stricter with him and insisted that he be confined with him and Daisy to the bedroom.

Phyllis, however, had other ideas and soon made it clear that she thought it unreasonable and unmanageable for them all to be together in that one room. Edwin was unwilling to listen to her and cross words brought tension to the household for a while. Phyllis was not unduly soft with the boy for, as Sheila put it, "Everyone could see that he was running wild at that time."

Events overtook them

A few weeks went by and in Hampshire they were waiting with growing anxiety for a decision from Woodford. Daisy was deteriorating fast so Phyllis wrote to explain the urgency of the situation.

However, events soon overtook them all as Daisy developed gangrene and was admitted to Winchester

Hospital to have her leg amputated, a procedure from which she never recovered. She died aged sixty on March 27th 1951 just a few weeks before Bev was admitted to Mill Grove. Scrawled across one of the letters in his file are the terse words, 'Action 19.3.51 Admit 9.4.51.'

Edwin wrote with sadness on March 28th, the day after his wife's death, accepting the place for Bev:

> *"Please excuse delay but Mrs Froud has been lying seriously ill and I am sorry to say she passed away yesterday.*
>
> *I note your instructions that Beverley can be admitted in your Home on the 9th April and accordingly arrangements have been made for him to be brought to you.*
>
> *My representative will be my very good friend, Mrs Savage, at whose address I am staying for a while. This lady has my complete confidence and can confirm everything regarding Beverley for actually she is the lady who cared for Beverley during the first five years of his life."*

This is the first mention of the Savages by name in any correspondence that has been preserved.

My first ever memory of Bev dates back to this time. I was standing with another boy near the gate of the recreation ground in Bishopstoke when he pointed Bev out to me. "That poor nipper, 'is mum's just died", he said. Of course, Daisy Froud was not his mother but, even if I'd known it at the time, how could I, an eleven year old, begin to understand or explain who she was and the nature of their relationship? He was somebody's son, but whose was clear only to very few people.

> **He was somebody's son, but whose was clear only to very few people.**

Changes for everyone

Edwin never did return to live in the bungalow in Chandlers Ford. The Savages helped him to clear his things and he continued to live in their home as a permanent lodger until he died just over three years later.

In May that year he visited Mill Grove with Phyllis and Wilfred for the first annual 'Our Day' celebrations at which Bev was present and took part. He wrote to the Director later that month:

> *"Firstly I must thank you for the very cordial greeting offered to my friends and myself, and for your very kind expression of sympathy at the death of my dear wife. I also want to say how glad I am that the Lord has placed Beverley in your care ... I am profoundly impressed, and no words can explain how pleased we all are to know that Beverley is now in such good hands and that his chance, so long delayed and interrupted is now at hand, and as far and as long as I can I shall fully give my support, for him, and others, for without a shadow of doubt, the work is a Glorious and Holy task.*
>
> *I wanted to see you to give you my cash ... I soon found that you were far too busy for matters of that kind. I do however enclose the first two months payment, as arranged, and for a humble thanksgiving offering for what I saw I enclose a further small sum, not a great deal, but sincerely given.*
>
> *I want to see you on a suitable occasion to give you the complete history of Beverley, for I know quite well, that it has been a puzzling case to you, but really it is too long an explanation to put in writing, and it is only right that you should have the full account."*

It is doubtful that a fuller account was ever given. Edwin sent £6 with his letter since, prior to her death, Daisy had agreed with him to pay the sum of 10 shillings a week for Bev's support, a sum he continued to send until his death. Later he wrote:

> "I am so glad to hear of Beverley's progress and I hope and pray it will continue ... Both Mr & Mrs Savage and I received a letter telling us the glad news that Beverley has been awarded the FP Stevens Memorial Bible. That in itself must be no mean achievement, but best of all it shows that all our prayers and the love and care imparted to him by your good-self and helpers have borne fruit far in excess of our expectation, and we all pray that it will continue to do so, and in the end Beverley will be an outstanding active and forceful 'messenger'."

Phyllis now takes up the writing for in June 1954 she reports that Edwin has been diagnosed with cancer:

> "He is finding great difficulty in walking. I'm afraid the news isn't very good. He has to go for Deep Ray treatment starting Monday ... I'm wondering how Beverley will face up to all this. I would like you to advise regarding having him here for his holiday ... We would like Beverley to have a holiday, and yet we wouldn't want him to see Mr. Froud suffer."

In fact, Bev did visit Bishopstoke that summer as he had done during previous long summer school holidays and recalls that Edwin, now very weak and mostly confined to bed, struggled to sit up so that he could play 'The Lord's my Shepherd' on his one-string fiddle. In October Phyllis wrote:

> "I have to tell you that Mr Froud passed away last evening (Saturday). It was very sudden in the end and even the Doctor was surprised. His end was very

// We all pray that in the end Beverley will be an outstanding and forceful 'messenger'.

> **His longing to be somebody's son was to be fulfilled ... he could think of none better to be his parents than those who had loved him from the beginning.**

peaceful, and he had a lovely smile on his face. I have written to Beverley and said his Daddy wasn't so well, but have left it to you to tell him this news. I don't know how things will stand concerning Beverley's keep at the Home. We must go into that together. Sufficient to say this is his home when he leaves school if he wants to come ... PS I will let you know the day of the funeral, but please don't let Beverley come home."

So, Edwin died in Scotter Road, Bishopstoke, where Phyllis and Wilfred nursed him until the end. The funeral service was held in their home since the church they attended did not have a permanent building until the following year.

Edwin's unexpected involvement with the Savages and with a child who was not his own, led him at last to place his faith in Jesus Christ in whom he now rests in peace.

These three, Edwin Froud and Phyllis and Wilfred Savage, although not related to Bev in any way, nevertheless provided an anchor and security for him during his early troubled years. It was no surprise then that when he heard of Edwin's death he asked the Savages whether he could call them Mum and Dad from then on, a request they were only too happy to receive and to answer positively.

His longing to be somebody's son was soon to be fulfilled and he could think of none better to be his parents than those who had loved him most from the beginning.

Chapter 14
INTO CARE

On the 9th April 1951, as arranged, Phyllis travelled to South Woodford with Bev beside her to begin his new life. Phyllis took him because Edwin was so recently bereaved and already struggling to cope with his own ill health. It must have been a bitter sweet day for her.

It did not seem to occur to anyone that Bev should remain with the family in Scotter Road. Everyone had been intent on finding a place for him to go and Edwin seemed to think of Phyllis and Wilfred simply as those who were employed to care for Bev in his infancy and kind friends who had helped them through their troubles.

Although it must have been a huge upheaval in his life, Bev has little memory of that journey. He just seems to have been told that he was going somewhere else to live.

"How did you feel about it?" I asked him. "I don't remember", he said. "I can only guess. You know how it would have been with me, excited, like going on an adventure, probably noisy, and underneath it all sick and scared, I imagine."

As the train slowly steamed into London Waterloo station he caught sight of the Festival of Britain

> God intended it for good to accomplish what is now being done, the saving of many lives.

exhibition on the South Bank of the river Thames with its signature Skylon, a suspended futuristic-looking, slender cigar-shaped steel structure pointing into the sky. The Festival was opened officially by King George VI the following month. He pleaded with Aunty Phyllis to go and see it but she hurried them on their journey down into the London Underground network and on to Woodford, there to meet the Director of Mill Grove.

Herbert White was seventy three years old when they met him that day in the front room of number 10 Crescent Road. He had been committed to the care of children in need for over fifty years. He himself had been orphaned at the age of thirteen and could no doubt look back with Joseph, and say of that experience, "God intended it for good to accomplish what is now being done, the saving of many lives."

How Mill Grove began

Herbert was a Sunday school teacher in Woodford Baptist Church, George Lane, when he came across Rosie, a nine year old girl with no shoes. She was crying because her mother had just died and Herbert took pity on her and enlisted the help of Rosa Hutchin, another unmarried member of the church, to look after her. Rosa took her home to live with her in her three roomed flat near the church and by April 1900 there were six girls being cared for by Ma Hutchin, as she became known.

When the flat was no longer large enough to accommodate them all, they moved into rented property in Latchett Road and then, in 1901 into houses in Crescent Road. One house was rented at first and then two more were built which also became available to rent. In 1930 the three houses were bought and presented to the charitable Trust that had been set up as the 'Home for Destitute and Motherless Children'. Later, halls were built and additional property added and over the years all were remodelled and integrated to make the premises the warm and welcoming complex that it is today.

Ma Hutchin was responsible for the day-to-day running of the home with just five or six helpers from her own family and from that of Herbert and Edith White and soon boys were received into care as well as girls. Herbert himself watched over the finances and administration and, when he and Edith had been married for just a brief time, they both agreed that he should resign from the Midland Bank in order to give himself fully to the work of the Home and to his calling to be an evangelist. It was 1907 and he was just twenty eight years old.

Living by faith

Herbert, their firstborn son, arrived at that time and this young family, with increasing responsibilities for the care of children, began to experience what it meant to live entirely by faith in God's provision for them all. Herbert and Edith went on to have six children of their own and, during the last century, over 1000 children have passed through the care of the White family. Still today, one hundred years later and two generations on, children are being rescued from neglect, desertion and the effects of bereavement through the work of Mill Grove.

The objects of the Home laid down at the beginning continue to be honoured and, in addition to their care, children are still introduced to the story of salvation that comes through faith in the life, death and resurrection of the Lord Jesus Christ, and lives continue to be changed by the love and grace of God.

An awe inspiring figure

To ten-year-old Bev, Herbert White was an awe inspiring figure of authority before whom he felt very nervous. The only memory that he has of that first meeting is of Pa White, as he was known, asking him to stand in front of him and to show him his hands after which he commented, *"Yes. I think we'll be able to make something of you."* Did he mean by that he could see a future for him in manual labour?

That was the expectation for children who went into care in those days in fact the 'Crescent Tea and Coffee Company' was formed by the Home to give youngsters work experience and help prepare them for life beyond care. When the Home was evacuated, some of the young people who were ready to leave care worked in the famous Wilkins Jam Factory which still exists in Tiptree today.

Name change

Although Herbert White had made it clear that they would revert to using Bev's registered name of Fletcher, Edwin did not easily give up on the matter. He wrote:

"The name on the Registration Card and Ration Card is Beverley Fletcher. May I emphasize this point a little - Beverley thinks his name is Froud, and if it is at all possible, we should like this to remain so, for we are certain that if it is known otherwise, Beverley would grieve very much, for young as he is, he has very strong ideas about his name being anything else but Froud. With regard to Mr Fletcher's name being on the certificate we are not able to state why this is so, as of course several years had gone before we knew anything of the matter at all."

In reality Bev did not seem to find it strange that

his name was suddenly changed when he went to Mill Grove neither does he remember strongly objecting to it. It seems that children at that time who were subject to many bewildering experiences just accepted that this was the way the world was. Once again he seemed to take changes on board without asking any questions and he doesn't remember anyone explaining the change to him.

Neither does he recall being upset when Phyllis left him that day but he has a clear memory of spending his first night in a dormitory with eight or nine other boys on the top floor of one of the houses in Crescent Road. He lay awake unable to sleep, excited and afraid, no doubt. He watched as 'flashes of lightning lit up the sky' and added to his fears. Actually the flashes were not lightning at all but came from the London underground electric trains as they negotiated the points at junctions, something he had never seen before.

The next day Herbert White drove him in his legendary Hillman to join the small number of children who were living at The Grove in Tiptree.

Flashes of lightning lit up the sky.

Chapter 15
THE GROVE

For over thirty years the White family and their helpers had been praying for a place to which they could send children to recuperate after illness and where larger groups could enjoy a holiday together. Some of the children who came to them in earlier years were malnourished and needed country air and fresh food to restore their health.

It wasn't until 1938, however, that their prayers were finally answered and a large and gracious double fronted house in the village of Tiptree was given to them. It was named 'Windmill Hall' probably after one of the prominent features in the village but was subsequently renamed 'The Grove'. Although it was some fifty miles from Woodford, it was just eight miles from the river Blackwater at Malden, a wide tributary that empties into the North Sea some five miles away.

A perfect location
The Grove proved to be a perfect location for the Mill Grove Family. There it enjoyed the delights of the country and had many memorable outings to the seaside too. At the beginning of their occupancy of the house and the various farm buildings adjacent to

it, the facilities were somewhat basic, to say the least, but nevertheless the gift came at just the right time as war broke out soon afterwards.

The village school, Tiptree Heath, provided for all ages so children from the home could remain there together until it was time for them to leave school.

One group was on holiday at The Grove in 1939 when war was declared and so their holiday home became their permanent residence for the duration of hostilities. The house and adjoining farm proved to be a particularly timely provision of God, for the Family was able to avoid the evacuation process operative in London which could easily have seen it scattered across the country with children and staff far from each other.

As it was, they remained together and unharmed in Tiptree until after the war when some children were taken back to Woodford under the care of Herbert White, while others remained in Tiptree under the supervision of Jean and Ewart White, Herbert and Edith's second son and his wife.

Behind the house were the farm buildings that had once housed sixty children, and beyond that were acres of farm land. Herbert White junior, who worked the farm with his wife and two daughters, lived in a bungalow a couple of fields away from the main house. It was quite common for wildlife to invade The Grove from time to time despite the best efforts of the staff to keep it out. This became more of a challenge as fewer children were placed there and less of the property was in regular use.

Sister Dorothy from Bishopstoke was there to welcome Bev when he arrived. There were just fifteen children in the house at this time and, although he hadn't known Dorothy well, it was a comfort to recognise at least one familiar face in the crowd of strangers.

He luxuriated in being with a group of children who could run and play safely without the ever present suffocating scrutiny of grown-ups.

Freedom to roam

He immediately relished the freedom and space of The Grove after years of confinement and luxuriated in being with a group of children who could run and play safely without the ever present suffocating scrutiny of grown-ups. The open air life was just what he needed and even the long walk to school was a dream; down the lane beside the stream and through the fields in which were growing the famous Wilkins Jam factory strawberries, past the little shop that sold broken biscuits for a half-penny and over the railway line along which ran 'the crab and winkle', reputed to be the slowest and rarest train on the planet and which few had ever witnessed first-hand.

The Grove was to some extent self-sufficient with its own produce and a kitchen garden from which vegetables were sent to Woodford. There was Blossom the horse and pigs and a windmill dominated the skyline north of the village. A small

lake across the road from the main house was the
scene of many a childhood adventure and the copse
with its tall pine trees, to the left of the drive into the
house, was an irresistible challenge to children who
loved to climb.

Memories of life at The Grove

The memories of those who lived there in 1952 are
packed with images of the 'ghost house' the children
built in a shed adorned with cobwebs and a bowl
of water set in the ground for unsuspecting visitors
to step into. There were games in the back field in
the long summer evenings and the memory of red-
haired Barry running panic stricken with his clothes
and hair singed by the fire that was boiling up
vegetable peelings to feed the pigs.

Bev recalls how his thumb nail was cut neatly
and deeply across the quick when the blade of a
lawn mower was pushed over it. The village doctor
ensured he would never be forgotten when, without
warning, he casually ripped off the remains of the
nail when it became infected. The visiting village
dentist was little better. He removed one of his teeth
but left a small splinter of tooth behind to cause him
sudden toothache every time he happened to touch
it. Daisy would have had something to say about all
this, no doubt, but in his new world the boys simply
delighted in retelling and embroidering these and
many other stories, real and imagined, as they lay
awake in the dormitory at night before dropping off
to sleep.

The Family attended the Congregational Church
on Sunday mornings but the older children counted
it a special treat when Sister Dorothy obtained
permission to take them to the northern end of the
village on Sunday evenings to the Salvation Army
Hall. The lively band and the enthusiastic worship

of the villagers was much more appealing than the rather staid worship of the decent Chapel folk.

It is not particularly easy for me to write of Bev's time in Mill Grove. I have been helped in recounting other periods of his life by the shared memories of the Savage family, but when he was in Tiptree and Woodford he was, in some senses, alone and his own memories of that time are hazy.

Memories are stirred and reinforced by stories recounted by our siblings, parents, aunts and uncles, by shared photographs and items that have found their way into our homes almost by accident. They remind us of holidays, weddings, visitors and other shared family experiences and most of us find that we are unable to distinguish between what we remember, what others in the family have told us or what we have simply absorbed over the years.

Occasional flashbacks

For Bev there are occasional flashbacks, small glimpses of events and places half remembered. Occasionally he'll recall a small thing from his past and I'll say, "You've never told me that before." It is noticeable that he finds it hard to remember people's names and relationships when we revisit the scenes of his past life but this is hardly surprising when he attended four schools in four different places and lived in four different settings during his childhood. Understandably, he feels only half-connected to most people who figured in his youth while some of them remember him very well even though he passed through their world only briefly.

I do, however, have one insight into an incident which changed him significantly. In fact, it made such an impact on him that it shaped the rest of his life.

> **You've never told me that before**

Chapter 16
AT LAST - A FATHER

The story came to me quite unexpectedly from a lady named Ruby Martin, who wrote from Witham in Essex. She used to visit The Grove when Bev was there. Here is an edited version of her account of what happened.

"Early in the 1950s I took a post in the village of Tiptree in Essex as a nanny to three, soon to be four, boys. As a newly believing Christian I quickly took up the suggestion to make contact with the staff at The Grove Children's Home in the village so that I could meet with them and learn from them. Jean and Ewart White were responsible for the work in those days and soon there was a bond between us which grew and lasted many years.

Each week I had a whole day off and more often than not it was spent at The Grove, as were many evenings. I learned much of the Lord in those years, really enjoyed the company of the staff and worked alongside Jean and Dorothy in caring for the children.

On the occasion of the death of Herbert White, the founder of the work, I felt it a great honour to be asked to 'hold the fort' at The Grove while some of the older children accompanied the staff to Woodford

Would God hear my prayer if I spoke to him?

for his funeral service.

Among my duties that day was to supervise bedtime, which I really enjoyed doing. After the children were ready to go to bed I told them a story and, since I had recently discovered the account of Hagar and Ishmael in the Old Testament, and it had really come alive to me, I told it to them. It is a story of God's care for a mother and child in great distress and I remember finishing by saying, 'You see God loves boys and girls and He listens and hears when you pray whatever it is about, and He has the answer.'

They had been very attentive during the story and the prayer and I felt very pleased that I had been given such a good reception. I wasn't too sure what the response would be when I expected them to go to bed and settle down without a staff member present, and I can't remember now if I had any problems with that, but I do remember that as the others rushed upstairs, one boy lingered and sidled up to me.

He said, "Would God hear my prayer if I spoke to Him?" "Yes", I said confidently and added, "The stories in the Bible are just the way God wants to help us today." "I want to love Jesus; can I ask him to come into my heart?" "You can", I said. I was trembling as I thought, 'This is the first time I've ever been asked that question.' "I'm not going to ask Him now but I will sometime." Then he ran off to join his friends in the drawn-out process in which many children excel when getting ready for bed.

Just a few days later I was back at The Grove sharing in a Bible Study with the staff. When Sister Jean had finished her rounds she came down and said enthusiastically, "I've something to tell you. At bedtime Beverley told me he had prayed and asked Jesus into his heart, 'Just like Miss Ruby had said.'"

I can't say that I had forgotten the incident but it

wasn't at the forefront of my mind when, over forty years later, I joined a few thousand other people at an FIEC conference and noted the Reverend Beverley Savage on the platform. He looked to be a young minister full of enthusiasm and I was blessed by what he had to say. I didn't make the connection at the time but later, as I read some biographical notes on him in an FIEC publication, I realised who he was - young Beverley from The Grove.

In recent years it has been such a pleasure to meet Bev and Val at the annual FIEC churches gathering in Caister and to be present for Mill Grove's Centenary Service at Tiptree Congregational Church when he preached. As I listened I was amazed to discover what God has done through this needy little boy who I'd cared for one night and to whom I had simply told a Bible story all those years ago."

Bev was only eleven at this time so his response to what he heard was, of course, that of a child. But it was life-changing for him. He was affected enough to feel that he should do something immediately to show that he really meant his commitment to Christ and the only thing that he could think of was to get rid of his collection of American comics. Quite why he thought that was necessary even he's not sure now but he owned nothing else that he valued and could give, so parting with his comics was the only gesture he could make to demonstrate the seriousness of his commitment.

How had this change come about?

This happened during his first few months in care so I found myself wondering how it was that he came to such faith in Jesus Christ so soon after leaving Bishopstoke.

He had, of course, been taught the Christian faith by Sunday School teachers in Chandlers Ford and

> I was amazed to discover what God has done through this needy little boy who I'd cared for and to whom I had simply told a Bible story all those years ago.

from time to time by the Methodist teachers in
Bishopstoke, but no one would have known that
their efforts were having any effect on him. His
behaviour was getting worse rather than better and
he was becoming adept at lying and stealing. His
future did not look promising. He certainly wasn't
born religious, so what happened to change him?
Let him tell you what he can remember of that
experience.

Bev's recollections

"As far as I can recall I first became aware that
something was wrong within me during the very
first night that I spent in Mill Grove. I remember
lying awake in the dormitory, watching flashes of
light across the sky and thinking that it was my bad
behaviour that had taken me there and that being
put in a Home was a punishment for the trouble that
I had brought to my family. I was overwhelmed by
the thought and silently cried into the night.

I realise now, of course, that much of what I felt
then came from my childlike interpretation of
all that had led to that point. It would be fair to
conclude that I was more sinned against than sinning
throughout my early life, but that is far from the
whole truth. I had really behaved badly and had
made a nuisance of myself making life difficult
for those who cared for me. Wrapped up in all the
confusion of that night I felt a pressing need to be
forgiven.

I can't say that those feelings continued to be at
the forefront of my mind in the following weeks,
preoccupied as I was with finding my way into an
entirely different world, trying to make new friends
and to fit into my substitute 'family', but they never
left me.

Part of my new routine was to assemble with

everyone else to read the Bible and pray each day and soon I began to appreciate just how important this was to the family that quite simply depended on God to supply absolutely everything it needed. As children we took it for granted that He would answer our prayers and would send supplies.

So, as the weeks turned into months and the daily readings and influence of the staff made their impression on me, I was unwittingly prepared for the commitment I would make.

Of all the places where I might have been sent, I came to Mill Grove, where Christ is known and loved and where I came to know him personally. I will never understand why that should have been, but I will be eternally grateful for it.

The story of Hagar that affected me so much continues to resonate with many who find themselves in need. In May 2017 Keith White, the grandson of the founder of Mill Grove and its present Director, stood in the same pulpit in Tiptree where I had once preached, to tell Hagar's story once again to the extended family of Mill Grove that had gathered for another 'Our Day' and, in his introduction, mentioned its significance to me all those years ago.

I have sometimes wondered about the genuineness of my commitment to Christ being so young, impressionable and needy, but after over sixty years of Christian experience I have no doubt that what happened to me at that time is explained by the New Testament when it says that true Christianity, the kind that changes people's lives for good and forever, is something that only God can do. It says,

"... God, who is rich in mercy, because of His great love with which He loved us, even when we were dead in trespasses, made us alive together with Christ ... For by grace you have been saved through

Somebody's son had a Father at last - and what a Father!

faith, and that not of yourselves; it is the gift of God …"*

My childlike response was by far the smaller part of what actually happened those many years ago. I started life again with God as my Father because He chose to adopt me as his son.

Somebody's son had a Father at last – and what a Father!"

Chapter 17

MILL GROVE

Christmas 1951 was Bev's first in the care of Mill Grove and was spent in Woodford. Children from The Grove joined those in Woodford for the celebrations, a coming together of the family that heralded the closure of The Grove in the following summer.

The occasion was made all the more memorable because it was the last Christmas when the voice of the founder, Herbert White, would be heard.

One, two, three, open!

Everyone gathered on Christmas morning as they usually did in the 'top hall', the space in which the Home's community events are held. They waited for Pa White to conduct them through the familiar programme of the morning, the centre piece of which was the opening of presents. But this Christmas Herbert was too ill to join them in person and so he spoke to them over a personal address system from number 10.

Everyone sat very still as he shared the Christmas story with 'his children'. It was like listening to the King's speech. He ended his talk true to his calling as an evangelist by appealing to all to place their

> The impact of his life and influence and the fruit of his devotion, lives on in the lives of thousands of 'his children' and their offspring.

faith in the Lord Jesus Christ. Then he pronounced the words for which every child had been waiting patiently, "One - two - three - OPEN!" That was the signal for everyone to unwrap their presents simultaneously and for festivities to begin.

Herbert White died in March 1952. His body was carried into the church by six of the young men who had been among 'his children'. He had given outstanding service to the cause of Christ and to the care of children for over fifty years and left behind him a remarkable example of what one man can accomplish when God is with him.

Dr D M Lloyd-Jones had once said, *"I do hope that someone will be able to prevail upon Mr White to write a book, not only of his experiences, but particularly upon the teaching which he feels is to be derived from what God has done through him."* He never did do that, but the impact of his life and influence and the fruit of his devotion, still lives on in the lives of thousands of 'his children' and their offspring who were cared for in Mill Grove, Bev among them.

Ma Hutchin had died ten years earlier in Tiptree aged seventy four having mothered some six hundred children.

Changes within the family

In the world of child care, the 1948 Children Act was to have a lasting impact on the development of services, both local authority and voluntary. Until the 1950s the numbers of children cared for at Woodford meant that the place had something of the scale and feel of an institution. There were as many as eighty nine children in the Home at the beginning of 1933, all wearing uniform, and even in the fifties Bev remembers wearing baggy khaki shorts and matching shirts in common with the other boys.

With Herbert's death the role of Director of Mill

Grove passed to Victor White, the youngest son in the family. He had returned from India at the end of the war and, with his wife Margaret, worked full-time in the Home. He had been chosen by his father as his successor and his appointment heralded many significant changes.

Victor and Margaret began to make Mill Grove less formal than previously and under their care children wore less regimented clothing and experienced greater freedom in relating to the wider community. Summer holidays were taken in such faraway places as Churston Ferrers, Torbay, Devon.

Bev benefitted from these changes and took advantage of the opportunities to join the Boys Brigade at the local Baptist Church and attend a Bible Class there.

He was especially excited when, at St Barnabas Secondary Modern School which he attended in Woodford, his name was pulled out of a hat and he joined thousands of London school children who lined the route at the Queen's Coronation in June 1953.

At that time a large banner was displayed on the outside wall of the top hall of the Home for all the neighbours to see. Alongside a picture of a Bible there was a quote from the Coronation Service itself, "Here is wisdom: this is the royal law: these are the lively oracles of God."

> Here is wisdom: this is the royal law: these are the lively oracles of God.

Losses and gains

There were many more children living in the Home in Woodford than in Tiptree when it closed so when the two groups were brought together the intimacy of the smaller group was diluted. St Barnabas School was also considerably larger than Tiptree Heath and Bev felt it to be overwhelming and impersonal at first.

The dense smog that engulfed London in the winter of 1952, thick, yellow and impenetrable, caused the deaths of up to eight thousand people in the city and added to Bev's sense of having lost something he had come to love in Tiptree.

However, the steady regularity of life in Mill Grove, the dedication of the staff and the new opportunities for engaging in the wider community contributed more to his life than he knew at the time.

Daily prayers continued and the whole 'Family' attended the Baptist Church each Sunday. As the children grew into their teens Victor White would take some of them with him to services in churches where he was preaching. In the autumn many of these would be Harvest Thanksgiving services. Dozens of churches would send their harvest display produce to Mill Grove and Bev has vivid memories of sitting on platforms at the front of congregations wedged behind harvest displays and, with others, eating his way through grapes and corn heads between hymns. Sometimes the youngsters themselves were encouraged to take part and he took several early steps in public reading and speaking at that time.

In May 1954 Dr Billy Graham, the famous American evangelist, held his first crusade in Britain at the Harringay Arena in North London. It was one of the most powerful of his crusades and members of the Mill Grove Family travelled to the meetings back and forth on the London Underground. Bev vividly remembers how the tunnels echoed to the sound of the popular hymns of the crusade, notably "Blessed Assurance, Jesus is mine".

Abridge Chapel
One of the lasting legacies left by Herbert White from his days as a travelling evangelist was a

small mission church which he had founded in the village of Abridge some five miles out into the Essex countryside. Children from the Home were often taken to services there and Arnold Gilbert led the church as honorary co-pastor with Herbert. He was a delightful grandfatherly figure who wore old fashioned wing collars and excelled as a storyteller. Olive, his wife and the eldest daughter of the White family, assisted him in the chapel and later worked tirelessly at Woodford alongside the staff.

The summer of 1955 was Bev's last in the Home and he asked to be baptized in the Abridge Chapel before he left. So one bright Sunday in June Mr. Gilbert baptised him along with a girl named Helena. It was to be Arnold's last service for next day the entire community was shocked when this much loved man suddenly collapsed and died. There is a memorial plaque in the chapel which commemorates the passing of Arnold Gilbert and also, incidentally, stands as a permanent reminder to Bev of his baptism.

When the time came for him to return to Bishopstoke, his Christian convictions were beyond question. He began to attend our local church with Wilfred, Phyllis and Sheila and joined our Young People's group bringing a freshness and openness with him which strengthened my own uncertain faith at the age of fifteen.

Changes in Hampshire

While he was away in Mill Grove there had been significant changes in Hampshire. The Foderinghams had moved from the bungalow in Chandlers Ford to a house in upper 'Stoke. Edwin Froud had died and Sheila was now married and living with her husband and baby son with Wilfred and Phyllis in Scotter Road, so the house was full again when Bev

Well you are our son, aren't you?

returned.

I asked Phyllis in her later years why it was that they agreed to take Bev back again when space was at such a premium. Looking directly at Bev she answered without a moment's hesitation, "Well you are our son, aren't you?" To her it was as simple as that, but it certainly could not have been easy for the family.

It is a huge tribute to them all that, in all the years I have known them, I have never once heard any complaint about Bev being there. Syd and Sheila went on living with Mum and Dad Savage until after their second child, a daughter, was born in 1958. Phyllis was in her early forties and Wilf was sixty years old when they found their house full of youngsters, but I get the impression that Wilf at least thrived on it.

Wilfred's journey of faith

Another very significant change that had occurred during Bev's absence was that Wilfred had also become a Christian. Apparently it happened when he reluctantly joined a Christian holiday group. As part of a game of hide and seek, a child was hiding stones on which were written Bible texts. Wilfred quietly picked one up and read of the love of God and that simple act began his search for the truth.

He was, of course, still the recognisable and loveable man he had always been but now his energy and boyish humour was directed to serving his Lord, the church and people of the village.

Wilf and Phyllis played a large part in the life of the church as its new building was erected and it employed its first full-time minister. Wilf became the caretaker of the building and well into his eighties he could be seen pushing his wheelbarrow up the hill to the church through the new housing estate, stopping to talk to anyone who would listen to him as he told them about his new found faith.

So Bev was home at last and a new stage of life began for him – and surprisingly it included me too.

Part 2

TO FIND A FAMILY
- A DIARY

Though my father and mother forsake me,
the Lord will receive me
Psalm 27:10

> *In less than a minute, months of speculation were brought to an end.*

Chapter 18

TAKING THE PLUNGE - JULY 2000

Calls to the police, funeral directors and crematoria, and perusing back copies of the Andover Advertiser, brought no answer to the question as to whether Bev's birth mother had been killed in a road traffic accident sometime between October 1999, when she was recorded on the electoral role, and July 2000 when we were searching for her. After a few weeks of frustration I needed to end the uncertainty.

Breakthrough

It was with some trepidation that I dialled the number listed for Lilian and Hector Fletcher's home which I found in a telephone directory. When the call was eventually answered I heard the voice of a frail old man, Hector Fletcher, I presumed.

I began simply by asking whether an LM Fletcher lived at that address and, without asking who I was, he told me that his wife had broken her hip earlier in the year and was now living permanently in a nursing home nearby. He named the area in which the home was located and, although it meant nothing to me at the time, I now had sufficient information to take the search forward. I thanked him and rang off.

> In one day I had found Bev's mother, a half-brother who had died and a half-sister alive.

In less than a minute, months of speculation were brought to an end. Both Hector and Lilian were still alive, but living apart.

Next, I called the Andover Information Office and found the receptionist very helpful. She was able to give me the telephone numbers of three homes in the area that Hector had mentioned and it wasn't long before I began to call them. At my second attempt I found her.

A Mrs Heron answered my call. She was the owner of the Nursing Home, and surprisingly forthcoming with information. As I scribbled furiously she revealed that Lilian had once had a son, Michael, who had died of a heart attack possibly in his forties and that her married daughter lived in the area and visited her mother regularly.

After several minutes of conversation, she suddenly seemed to become aware that she was acting unprofessionally and abruptly asked who I was. I replied that we were relatives who hadn't seen Lilian for some time – an understatement if ever there was one.

I kept the conversation going so that I could find out how well Lilian was and whether it might be possible for us to contact her if we ever thought that we would like to. She suddenly put me on the spot when she offered to give Lilian's daughter a message from me so I found myself saying to her that it would not be a good idea as it was a rather delicate situation. Much to my relief she was very understanding and said that I could ring her at any time and she would be willing to co-operate with me should I wish to take this any further.

In one day I had found Bev's mother, a half-brother who had died and a half-sister alive. I could hardly wait for him to come home so that I could share my success.

What now?

As the weeks passed and I accumulated more information so the dilemmas increased. With Lilian alive and living apart from her husband, might it now be possible to meet her face-to-face without causing him distress or affecting any other member of the family?

It could, of course, seriously backfire. She could suffer a heart attack from the shock or become so upset that soon everyone would know that we were responsible. At nearly ninety years of age it was quite possible that she no longer had any clear memories of Bev or may have lost the ability to even communicate. She could refuse to see him again as she had done when he was fourteen years old and I had no idea how that would affect him. So they could both be left worse off.

On the other hand it could result in them laying to rest issues from the past and enjoying at least a semblance of a mother-son relationship, however brief if might be, and that could bring healing and huge pleasure to them both.

Chapter 19
MEDIATOR - AUGUST 2000

It was mid-August and we were visiting some old friends to make arrangements to borrow their caravan the following month so that we could combine a holiday with visiting some churches in the flatlands of East Anglia. Over a meal I found myself recounting the story of our exploration into Bev's family history.

The revelation that his natural mother was still alive soon took the conversation beyond a detached account of our adventures to serious questions about what we planned to do in the light of what we had discovered.

Frank: advisor and mediator

Frank, now retired after a career in the probation service and then as a pastor, quickly grasped the complexities of the situation as we reflected on the prospect of making contact with Lilian. He talked us through the various options and then advised us that, if we really felt compelled to take matters further, it would be less stressful for everyone if we were to approach her through a third party. That way Lilian could take what time she needed to decide if

For all my experience I've never been involved in a situation quite like this before.

she wanted to meet us and, if she did not want to do so, the go-between would set her mind at rest before terminating the conversation and also soften the impact of the disappointment for us.

This immediately struck us as a sensible next step and we began to consider who among our friends we might choose for such a delicate task.

It took just a few minutes to conclude that Frank himself would be perfect for the role of a mediator. This caught him by surprise. "For all my experience," he said, "I've never been involved in a situation quite like this before." As we argued the case for his involvement he gradually softened and as we left that evening he and Bev agreed that they would both think and pray about the situation for the next few days and get in touch again.

As we drove home in the twilight through the Oxfordshire lanes we talked about Frank and the possibility of him representing us and as we did so our confidence in him grew. He seemed to be a gift to us. We smiled when we remembered that Frank was the only minister among our friends who still wore a clerical-collar, a useful badge of authenticity for an unknown minister visiting a nursing home.

It took a couple of sleepless nights to persuade Bev that we should approach Lilian and that Frank was the right person for the task. Having made the decision, he soon emailed Frank to confirm his request. On Monday August 14th, the day of Bev's sixtieth birthday, we found ourselves back in their home again talking through the practicalities and providing Frank with the background information he would need to answer at least some questions that Lilian might raise with him. As we left he agreed to 'phone the nursing home the next day to speak to Mrs Heron.

Contact - and complications

Tuesday proved to be a nerve-racking day. We rehearsed what the outcome of Frank's call could be and had further misgivings about whether we were doing the right thing. Mrs Heron was not available that morning but eventually Frank spoke to her in the afternoon. He found her very helpful but to his dismay she talked of calling in the Social Services for advice before she took matters further since she had never faced such a situation before and, understandably, felt that her primary responsibility was to protect Lilian.

Frank successfully concealed his alarm and gently persuaded Mrs Heron that this would probably not be the most appropriate way forward. He had considerable experience with Social Services and was anxious to avoid unnecessarily escalating the situation so that it became more complex and would lead, most likely, to involving other members of the family. However, Mrs Heron would not be dissuaded until, at last, a compromise solution was agreed. She would speak to Lilian's doctor instead and be led by his advice. This she did later that afternoon and his response was insightful. "This might be something that she needs", he said. "She has been rather depressed for several years."

So, with the doctor's permission and encouragement, Mrs Heron went to talk with Lilian and to tell her gently that someone was trying to contact her. Her first reported words were, "How peculiar!" Could it be that she had been thinking of Bev just a few days before on his birthday? Can a mother ever forget the day she gives birth?

Lilian clearly had her wits about her because, after some thought, she put three questions to Mrs Heron which she wanted answered before she would agree to respond further. "Ask him who he is, where he

How peculiar!

was born and how he knew that I was here?"

Mrs Heron, now thoroughly intrigued, soon telephoned Frank with the questions - and he was ready with the answers. "He is Beverley Savage. He was born in the New Forest in a place named Woodlands and he knows that you are here because he has been looking for you and found out about you from others." The details were soon relayed back to Lilian.

That evening Mrs Heron spent more time with Lilian talking about the day, the effect that Frank's enquiry had on her and how she was coping with this completely unexpected turn of events. Frank reported all of this to us while we hung breathlessly on his every word.

Tantalisingly, Mrs Heron was off duty for the next few days so it was not until Friday afternoon that we received the next instalment of the story from Andover. Those days seemed endless to us and we realised just how emotionally invested we had become in the outcome.

Bev welcomed the distraction of his work while I had time to imagine what might be going on in Lilian's mind and play out the possibilities of her reactions. Was she pleased, frightened perhaps, angry or maybe exasperated that something she thought she had left behind several decades previously was surfacing yet again? We had no way of knowing.

The call

Then came the telephone call for which we had been waiting. Bev took it in his office which was in another part of the house and came out to tell me. As soon as I saw him I knew something significant had been said. At first I was alarmed. Had this all gone badly wrong? I waited for Bev to speak. He was finding it difficult. Eventually he said that when Lilian heard Frank's responses to her questions, she said immediately *"Yes that's my son. I thought it would be."*

// Yes that's my son. I thought it would be.

He could hardly finish the sentence but when he had regained his composure he said, "You've no idea what those words mean for me." And, of course, I didn't. How could I understand what it felt like to have a mother acknowledge him as her own son for the first time since he was born 60 years earlier?

She was the first blood relative ever to acknowledge that he really belonged to the family.

There was no way we were going to be able to concentrate on anything else that day so we went out to eat and we talked and talked about what Frank had told us. I remember Bev's words so clearly that evening. "I feel strangely connected for the first time."

A deeply hidden need

Earlier that month in the course of Bev's work we spent a few days in Jersey. As we walked its beautiful sandy beaches, Bev had talked of his childhood memories more than he had ever done in the 45 years I had known him. It was then that he rather surprised me by saying that all his life he had felt a sort of 'non-person', not really belonging or fitting anywhere. That is why he moves on with comparative ease from one situation to another without putting down roots.

No one observing him in his adult life could have imagined that he felt that way. He appeared so at ease with himself, confident and able to cope with most situations. People look to him to lead, a teacher, someone who is there for them. Hadn't the Savage family loved him and been as caring as any family could be? Was that not more than sufficient compensation for the loss of his natural family? Apparently not.

There was a very deep and genuine love between him and Wilfred, Phyllis and Sheila. They were his family and no one could ever replace them. Yet an intensity of feeling overwhelmed him when a woman he had never known, who had appeared to abandon him and did not want to meet him, to whom he owed nothing, named him as her son.

Clearly there was within him a deeply hidden need to be owned by his own flesh and blood no matter how they had behaved towards him. Without that acknowledgement it seemed that he would always feel an outsider, a skeleton in the cupboard, a secret to be hidden, someone with a history to be concealed.

Chapter 20
FIRST VISIT - AUGUST 2000

After further careful preparations Lilian did agree to see Frank. She was very anxious that no-one should know of his visit and certainly no one should tell Hector. Frank was advised not to go into the nursing home in an afternoon or on a Saturday and Sunday as her daughter visited her mother at irregular times over the weekend.

This development encouraged us not least because both the doctor and Mrs Heron considered that Lilian was well enough to receive visitors. Her questions showed a keen mind and a curiosity. Were we wrong to dream that Frank could pave the way for more contact? Mrs Heron, now very concerned to do the right thing, asked Frank if he was sure that he had the right woman. "Oh yes", he said. We're one hundred percent sure."

His first visit took place on a Monday morning around 11am. He stayed only a short time so as not to tire Lilian or cause her stress. He left before the midday lunch was served and came straight on to our home to have a meal with us.

She spoke and we drank it in
The first thing he told us was that Lilian is a believer

> **She has had a sense of guilt for a very, very long time and has found it hard to believe that she could be forgiven.**

in the Lord Jesus Christ. We could hardly believe it. Apparently she had been a practising Anglican most of her life but in more recent years had felt that her church had little to give her. So she had begun to attend a small Baptist Church near her home and said that she would have liked to have been baptised there but her health would not allow it. "She has had a sense of guilt for a very, very long time," Frank said, "and has found it hard to believe that she could be forgiven."

Lilian shared many details of her life that day all of which Frank relayed to us and we drank it in. Lilian Fletcher, we now learned, had been the headmistress of a primary school in Tidworth, a military town on the borders of Hampshire and Wiltshire, one we passed through many times on our various journeys.

She would be eighty nine years old on Saturday August 26th and many of her family were planning to be present to celebrate the day with her. She spoke of her daughter who is a personnel officer in Andover and of grandchildren and great grandchildren, some of whom live in Plymouth, but she didn't mention her son, Michael.

We were particularly fascinated to learn that Lilian's father, Bev's grandfather, had been a railwayman in Cambridge but had gone on to become a councillor and a JP, and had received an OBE and an honorary degree from the University.

We were moved to hear Frank say that Lilian had never forgotten Bev. Never a year went by without her thinking of him particularly on his birthday, a date that was permanently etched on her memory because it was her father's birthday too.

She explained that she had always expected that the Frouds would adopt him. That is what Ted Foderingham had led her to believe as he attempted to reassure her that Bev would be well provided for. To me it seemed a remote possibility since they were in their fifties when they took Bev to live with them, but it was wartime and it was not unusual for orphaned children to be entrusted to the care of older people.

Lilian had been made aware that Bev would have to go into care because of Daisy Froud's deteriorating health and she told Frank that she had spent a lot of time trying to find a private boarding school for him but the costs were just too high. She knew of the Frouds' deaths and she had always imagined that Bev was in a large Dr Barnardo's Home somewhere. She confirmed, and expanded on much of what I had gathered from his file.

There were tears from her as Frank told her that her son had in fact gone to a small Christian home in Essex and there had become a Christian and later a Christian minister.

It sounded from his report that Frank had given her a rather glowing picture of Bev. After he had left, Bev remarked, "If she ever does agree to see me she'll probably be disappointed when her expectations have been raised so high."

We also heard how Hector Fletcher had been very supportive of her when her pregnancy was discovered and her affair with Ted Foderingham came to light. "He was a brick", she said. It was so strange to hear her actual words and each snippet felt as though we were getting just a little closer to knowing her.

It was the right time
We began to see the providence of God working in the timing of our approach to her. Our first reaction to discovering her so late in life was, 'if only we had been able to meet her sooner we would have got to know her better.' But the more we thought about

It would kill him.

it the more we could see that, had Lilian still been living at home with Hector, she certainly could not have agreed to any contact with us at all. He was frail and in his nineties now and Lilian herself said if he knew that we had been in touch, "It would kill him."

Lilian had a serious fall around Christmas 1999 and had broken her hip. The operation to repair it had been successful but she fell and broke it again and this time further surgery was ruled out because she was so frail. She was taken into the nursing home sometime in the spring of 2000 and had been given only two weeks to live. However, against all expectations she had pulled through and, although she spent her time in a wheelchair and needed constant assistance, it seemed to us that she had been spared so that we could meet her and she could perhaps set the past to rest.

A positive start

There were already some very positive benefits for Lilian and for Bev from this initial meeting even though it was through an intermediary. Lilian was reassured that things had worked together for good in her son's life despite his difficult start. Frank told her that Bev had no bitterness towards her and found no difficulty in forgiving her for all that had happened.

It was obvious to Frank that Lilian found great relief in talking to him about the painful memories that she had kept to herself for many years and his Bible reading and prayer with her also brought her comfort.

For Bev it was an amazing gift to know that his mother shared his Christian faith, that she had not forgotten him and that she really had cared about what had happened to him.

Canadian connection

Should she ever agree to meet Bev?

During the course of their conversation Lilian mentioned a Canadian lady who had been working with the small Baptist church at the end of the road in which she had lived. She had visited Lilian and Hector in their home and Lilian found her to be someone to whom she could talk easily. I wondered whether it would be helpful for the two of them to meet again. Perhaps Lilian would find it a release to share news of our contact with a comparative stranger who had no other links with her family.

Frank's visit had obviously raised important issues for her and posed some very difficult questions. Should she agree to our continued contact with her, running the risk of her lifelong secret being discovered by her family? Should she ever tell her daughter that she had a half-brother just eleven months older? And the most difficult question of all, should she ever agree to meet Bev?

I made enquiries and discovered that Lenore, the Canadian lady in question, was working with an American church group in the UK with which Bev already had close contact. I telephoned her and learned that we had met her some months previously when she, with other members of her group, had attended a conference that Bev had organised in another part of the country. I discovered that she was soon to leave Andover and, after a period back in the USA, was then to be reassigned to another town in Britain.

Without disclosing the reason for my request, I asked if she would be willing to visit Lilian again. I hoped that Lilian would feel freer to confide in her knowing that she would soon be gone from the area. She readily agreed to my suggestion but, disappointingly, when she visited her, Lilian simply told her of an unexpected visit from a Baptist minister and that, "There is a secret which I will, perhaps, tell you about when you return from America." It was never to be.

Lenore called to reassure me that Lilian seemed in good spirits, not unduly distressed or agitated, and that she was looking forward to the family get-together for her birthday the next day.

She went on to enlarge on her experience of visiting the Fletcher household which she had been doing for some years. From her I learned that Hector appeared to be indifferent to the Christian faith and would leave the two women to talk together in the front room. He had lost part of one arm during the war but was managing well on his own, supported by his daughter and his daughter- in-law, Michael's widow. A grand-daughter also visits her grandparents regularly.

Lenore spoke of Lilian's alert mind and positive attitude to the nursing home where she is living. She is grateful for all that is done for her there though she is frustrated that she can no longer walk. She thought that Michael, Bev's half-brother, had died possibly around 1991 when he would have been around 54 years of age.

Chapter 21

SECOND VISIT
- AUGUST 2000

Frank next visited the nursing home on Tuesday August 29th. This time Lilian seemed to feel the need to talk to him about their son Michael whom she hadn't mentioned previously.

Frank gradually formed the impression of a charming and morally upright woman who was concerned to be straightforward and honest and not to leave things unsaid that needed to be faced. Yes, Michael had died suddenly in his mid-fifties. He had three children while his sister had a son and daughter and two grandchildren. She visits her mother every day as she works near-by and calls in on her way home.

The affair

Lilian spoke quite openly of her relationship with Bev's father whom she called Teddy. It was an affair rather than a fleeting intimacy. Frank asked her whether she was in love with him and she replied, still with a sparkle in her eyes, "Oh yes, very much so". She described him as, "A fine man but unreliable, a man who told fairy tales".

Frank told her that Bev had characteristics from both of them - his father's charm and her uprightness. He also mentioned in passing that Bev is quite dark-skinned and she said that Teddy was too, but she had always assumed that he was English since she had no reason to think otherwise. It was only later that she heard that Teddy's father was probably from abroad.

Hector was Teddy's boss and both were based in the Winchester office of the Liverpool Victoria Friendly Society. She said that the two of them visited her together in the nursing home when Bev was born, although it seemed to me unlikely unless, of course, Ted had driven him there. I could only guess what kind of journey that might have been for them both.

Lilian also said that they had taken Michael to see the baby and that there were photographs of the two boys together. This again I found hard to imagine. It went against all our preconceptions that the baby was taken away from her quickly so that she would not bond with it.

I wondered if Lilian knew how long Bev had remained in the nursing home until he was taken to be 'put out to nurse' with Mrs Savage but she gave no indication that she was aware of the details of

what happened to him after she had last seen him. Apparently she had no photographs of him since Hector had meticulously erased all evidence that the pregnancy and birth had ever taken place.

On this visit Frank had taken a photograph of Bev and me together and on seeing it she had immediately remarked, "He looks very like his father".

At one point in the conversation Frank suggested gently that Bev might pop in to see her one morning as he himself had done, but she didn't respond. It seemed that she needed more time to come to terms with what was happening and to work out how to handle it.

However, before Frank left, Lilian did say, "Tell Beverley I love him and would love to see him, but it can't be - not now." What she meant by that was not clear to us. Did she mean that she could not see him while Hector was alive or was she closing the door for ever? Understandably, she was concerned that her daughter would discover that Frank had been visiting her although he had been very careful to cover his tracks by signing the visitor's book as someone visiting the owner of the Home, Mrs Heron, which in fact he did each time he went.

Mrs Heron confided to Frank that she had spoken to Lilian suggesting that, knowing what a good relationship she had with her daughter, she should confide her secret to her but Lilian made it very clear that she could not contemplate raising the subject with any of her family.

So little by little it became clear that it was unlikely that we would ever meet her. It was tantalising but entirely understandable. She was so near and yet still beyond our reach.

> Tell Beverley I love him and would love to see him, but it can't be - not now.

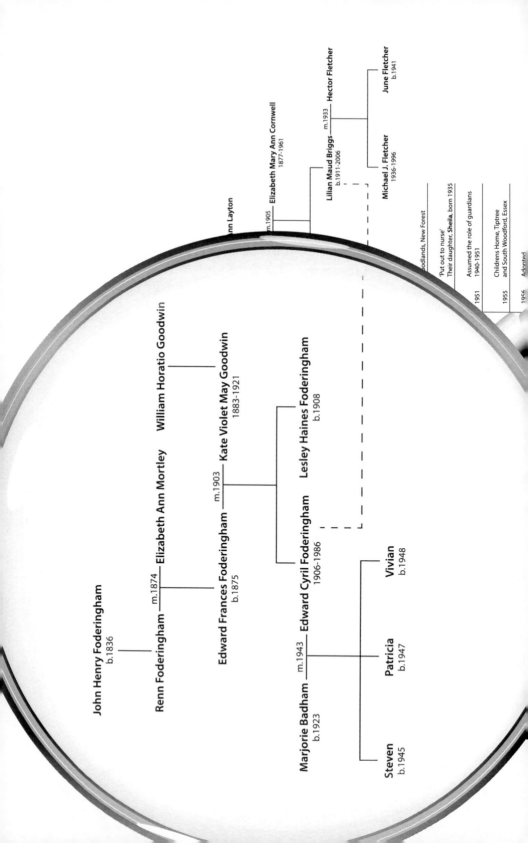

John Henry Foderingham
b.1836

Renn Foderingham —— m.1874 —— Elizabeth Ann Mortley   William Horatio Goodwin

Edward Frances Foderingham —— m.1903 —— Kate Violet May Goodwin
b.1875   1883-1921

Marjorie Badham —— m.1943 —— Edward Cyril Foderingham   Lesley Haines Foderingham
b.1923   1906-1986   b.1908

Steven   Patricia   Vivian
b.1945   b.1947   b.1948

...nn Layton

...m.1905   Elizabeth Mary Ann Cornwell
                   1877-1961

                   Lilian Maud Briggs —— m.1933 —— Hector Fletcher
                   b.1911-2006

                                                    June Fletcher
                                                    b.1941

                   Michael J. Fletcher
                   1936-1996

...oodlands, New Forest

'Put out to nurse'
Their daughter, Sheila, born 1935

Assumed the role of guardians
1940-1951

1951

        Childrens Home, Tiptree
        and South Woodford, Essex

1955

        Adopted

1956

Chapter 22

GRANDFATHERS
- SEPTEMBER 2000

"I think I may have found both of your Grandfathers!"

It was one lunch time in September. Bev had been working in his office all the morning and I had been thinking about our forthcoming break using Frank and Betty's touring caravan.

We had talked about spending some time in Winchester during the first weekend searching the microfilm records for more Foderingham family details. I rang the Records Office just to check that they would be open on the Saturday and while I was speaking to them it occurred to me to ask whether they held any records there of men who had served in the Merchant Navy. I had previously discovered Edward Foderingham's date of birth and had sent for a copy of his birth certificate. This confirmed that Kate May Foderingham, a name I had previously found in the records, was indeed Ted's mother and that his father was Edward Francis, a Quartermaster in the Merchant Service. At the time of Ted's birth in 1906 they were recorded as living in Shirley, Southampton.

The helpful receptionist at the Records Office gave me the telephone number of the Southampton

> **We had, indeed, found the right man and the right address at the very first attempt.**

Archives Service and, when I called, an archivist immediately offered to look for any information they might hold on the first Edward Foderingham. I discovered that they held identity cards that record details of all those who had served in the Merchant Navy. She suggested I ring back in an hour or so.

Meanwhile I rang the Cambridge Records Office. Our forthcoming tour was to include visits to churches in the Norfolk and Cambridgeshire areas and I thought that, while we were there, we could research Lilian's family.

We knew from Bev's birth certificate that her maiden name was Briggs and, coupled with the information that Lilian had given Frank about her father of whom she was obviously very proud, I thought that we had a good chance of tracking him down.

The Records Office was again very helpful and, as the receptionist was talking to me about the various sources that might be useful to us, he suddenly asked what dates I thought Mr Briggs might have been on the Council in Cambridge. I was rather put on the spot so just floated some dates, "Oh I suppose it might be sometime in the thirties or forties."

He left the 'phone for a moment to reach for a book on one of the shelves nearby. He pulled out a copy of Kelly's, an annual record of many of the residents in the city of Cambridge. "Well!" he said, "I have here the copy of Kelly's for 1937 and there's an Alderman William Layton Briggs, a JP, living at that time in Mill Road. It's in a rather commercial part of town and at one time there had been a hairdresser's at that address."

I detected in his voice a slight surprise that a man from that area should hold such offices. This certainly could be the Briggs I was looking for, though I had no way of knowing for sure. It wasn't until I later sent for a copy of Lilian's birth certificate that I realised that we had, indeed, found the right man and the right address at the very first attempt. This was hardly surprising since, as I was later to discover, he had been such a prominent person in Cambridge.

Later in the morning I was back in contact with the Archive Services in Southampton. The archivist had been busy on our behalf and was keen to share the information she had gathered.

"Yes", she said, "I've found an Edward Foderingham, no second name given. He is recorded as being a Bosun's Mate. He was 5'10" tall and was born in Barbados on October 6th 1875. He is listed as of British nationality. Could this be the person you're looking for?" I thought that it almost certainly was. The information corresponded with what Phyllis had told me only fairly recently, that 'a coloured gentleman' featured somewhere in Ted Foderingham's background.

Then to my amazement she went on to say, "There's even a photo of him here. And I've found another Foderingham - Leslie Haines Foderingham, born 1908 also from Southampton. There are also numbers and dates on one side of the card and names of the ships on which they served on the other. If you would like further information you will need to contact the Public Records Office at Kew."

I arranged for her to send me copies of the pink identity cards for these Foderingham men and as I replaced the receiver my mind was in a whirl.

Who was this second man? Could it be Ted's younger brother? In all my research I had found virtually no one else in the UK with the name Foderingham except for those who were living in the Southampton area all of whom were almost certainly connected to this man from Barbados.

The Foderingham connection

This led me to wonder how it was that the surname
Foderingham came to be so widely used in Barbados
when it sounded anything but West Indian.

I called a lady I had come across in a telephone
directory whose surname happened to be
Foderingham and who, I discovered, was also
looking into her husband's history. She had once
contacted a TV presenter after seeing a programme
on family heritage and he had told her that
Foderingham was most likely to have been an old
Scottish aristocratic family name.

Apparently, prestigious families with younger
members who misbehaved and threatened to
disgrace them, sent them off to the Caribbean
to manage estates where slaves were sometimes
given the name of their owners, replacing their
African names. So it is quite likely that the name
Foderingham had its origin here in Britain and
had been used to designate ownership of slaves in
Barbados.

So in one morning, with comparative ease, I had
discovered Bev's two grandfathers, and possibly
an uncle, and had probably identified the origin
of his father's surname. It was a lot to absorb and
I knew instinctively that Bev would need time to
come to terms with the revelation that his paternal
grandfather was a black West Indian man. Here
was an entirely new and unexpected twist to his
story, a revelation that would give him a whole new
perspective on his roots and identity.

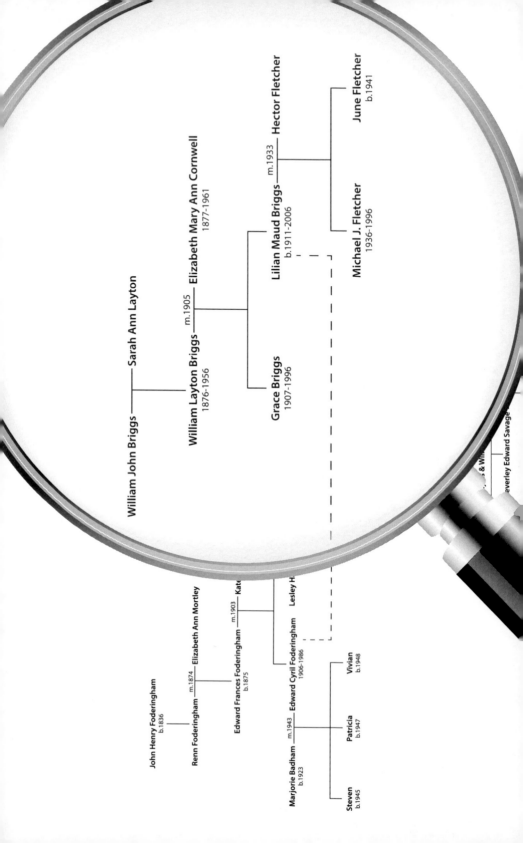

William John Briggs ———— Sarah Ann Layton

William Layton Briggs —m.1905— Elizabeth Mary Ann Cornwell
1876-1956   1877-1961

Grace Briggs
1907-1996

Lilian Maud Briggs —m.1933— Hector Fletcher
b.1911-2006

Michael J. Fletcher   June Fletcher
1936-1996   b.1941

John Henry Foderingham
b.1836

Renn Foderingham —m.1874— Elizabeth Ann Mortley
b.1875

Edward Frances Foderingham —m.1903— Kate
Edward Cyril Foderingham   Lesley H
1906-1986

Marjorie Badham —m.1943— Edward Cyril Foderingham
b.1923

Steven   Patricia   Vivian
b.1945   b.1947   b.1948

s & Wil
everley Edward Savage

Chapter 23

CAMBRIDGE
- SEPTEMBER 2000

We never did get to Winchester that first weekend of our holiday. Action by farmers and hauliers meant that there was suddenly no petrol to be had anywhere so it was Tuesday September 19th before we could leave home with the caravan.

We had several important engagements to fulfil on our way to Cambridge, including the wedding of our son Ian in Kent, but eventually we arrived and parked south of the City.

Being keen to start our investigations, we set out immediately for a quick tour of Cambridge. That was a mistake. It was the evening rush hour and the traffic was virtually gridlocked which almost derailed our plan to find Mill Road and the house where Lilian had been born and to take photographs of it before the evening closed in.

However, though it took much longer to find than we had expected, we eventually drew up outside the property and we stood before the very place where Bev's mother had been born eighty nine years earlier. The house had obviously been extended and modernised since the Briggs had lived there and it was now linked to the property next door

There was Alderman William Layton Briggs JP, OBE, MA in his full Mayoral regalia.

to accommodate a doctor's surgery. This part of Cambridge, known as Romsey Town, had always been one of the poorer parts of the City and small terraced houses and shops still characterise the area. We took our photographs and, since the evening traffic had thinned, had an easier return journey to the caravan tired but satisfied with our first foray.

Later that evening we rang Frank to find that he had visited Lilian for the third time and had more useful pieces of information for us, which I would carry with me as we headed into the City the next day.

We had decided that our starting point would be the Records Office in the Shire Hall. The process by which one is permitted access to records can be somewhat complicated but, once in, we were amazed, as we always were, by the huge amount of information that is meticulously stored and available to archivists. We had imagined that it would take hours of searching through ancient records to get the information we were looking for but as it happened we found what we needed very quickly.

Grandfather Briggs

We were sitting at a table in a library area and simply turned round to examine a shelf behind us where the Kelly's volumes were displayed. I picked out the one dated 1936 and, slowly turning the pages to get my bearings, I was suddenly surprised to come across a full plate photograph of Alderman William Layton Briggs JP, OBE, MA in his full Mayoral regalia! No wonder that Lilian was proud of him. Bev seemed awestruck as he looked for the first time into the face of his maternal grandfather to find that it was true, he had been a noteworthy figure in that great City.

Alderman Briggs had twice been mayor of Cambridge and later that day as we wandered through that world renowned seat of learning with its quaint streets and fine churches and colleges, we found ourselves almost proprietorial, proud that a true relative had been so honoured and appointed twice over to such a position of responsibility in that prestigious city.

From the Records Office in the Shire Hall we made our way to Great St Mary's church, the University church, opposite King's College. We read the information displayed outside which is of particular interest to evangelical Christians:

'There was a church on this site in the eleventh century. It was rebuilt in 1298, and the existing church, sponsored by the University, dates from 1478. For centuries Great St Mary's was used by the University for religious, academic and public functions. It was closely associated with the Reformation. Erasmus, Cranmer, Ridley and Latimer preached here. Bucer was buried here in 1551, but his corpse was exhumed and publicly burnt outside in Mary's reign. It is said that Oliver Cromwell had the Book of Common Prayer destroyed here in his presence. Although still used for university services Great St Mary's is also a parish church. The Mayor and Corporation have come here for civic services for many centuries.'

So Bev's grandfather had once processed into the church and attended its services as part of his civic duties.

Lilian had told Frank only the day before our visit that both her parents had been buried in the church but Frank was unsure that she had remembered that correctly. When we enquired about that, the officials in the ancient church took time to look up the records for us and rang the crematorium to discover that, while the funeral services of William Briggs and his

They were invited to the Coronation of King George VI.

wife had been held in the church, they had in fact been cremated and their ashes scattered.

From Great St Mary's we went to the Central Library and, with the help of the staff, uncovered a wealth of fascinating information about William and his wife, Elizabeth Mary Ann. There, on microfiche, were stored copies of newspapers containing numerous articles about them, often accompanied by photographs. There was extensive coverage of the grand ceremony at which William was recognised as Mayor in November 1936. We also found a record of their Golden Wedding celebrations in September 1955 and accounts of their funerals, first for William in 1957, and then Elizabeth in 1960. Both were accompanied by many fine tributes paid to them by notable people of the city and from the university.

We were left with the impression of a couple who had deep roots in a working-class area which they both served and in which they remained firmly embedded all their lives.

It appeared that 'Billie', as he was known by many, was at least the third generation of his family to live in the Romsey Town area and they were able to claim that "nearly everybody in Romsey knows us". Such was the extent of his service and influence in many spheres of public life that it was a claim that could well have been made for the entire City of Cambridge.

During their first period as Mayor and Mayoress, Alderman and Mrs Briggs were invited to the Coronation of King George VI. They wrote to apologise to His Majesty saying that they would like to spend the Coronation with their own people in Cambridge, a decision they never regretted for they had a wonderful time among those they served.

Lilian and her sister, Grace, were raised in the city in a fairly modest terraced house and, even when

Billie retired early from the railway in 1935 because of ill-health, they moved only a few streets away to a detached house in Greville Road.

William had been born in 1876 and had begun working on the railway when he was fifteen years old, just as his grandson, Bev, had done after him. On Lilian's birth certificate he is noted as being a store man, but by the time he retired he was Chief Clerk, a senior executive position.

Elizabeth had been born in Bury St. Edmunds a year later in 1877. Her family lived in Newmarket for a time but then, when she was fifteen, they too had moved to Cambridge. It seems that she lived fairly near to William because it is reported that they met when they were both involved in church work, Elizabeth as a Sunday School teacher in St Barnabas and St Philips' churches, both of which are in Mill Road.

They were sweethearts from around the age of nineteen but didn't marry until they were twenty nine and twenty eight years old respectively. This was because William had resolved that he wouldn't marry until he was earning at least £1.10s a week. In the event, after waiting ten years, he felt compelled to revise his ambition and marry Elizabeth at St Barnabas Church on September 27th 1905 despite the fact that his earnings were only £1.8s a week.

They worked in the community from an early age forming National Savings groups, Billie among the Cambridge railway employees and Elizabeth at Romsey School. Billie was said to be a pioneer of the Labour movement in Cambridge and was later to become chairman of the Romsey Labour group and a trade unionist within the Railway Clerks Association.

At the time of his inauguration as Mayor it was said that:

"There was a point just after the First World War

when he had to make a definite decision about whether he would devote his future life to the trade union world or work in his own town. The former held many attractions in the way of adventure, and perhaps some gratification for his fighting spirit, but he was thankful to know that in the path he chose he had been able to find full scope for serving his fellow men."

*Briggs has been a member of the Town Council since
1920 and was elected Alderman in 1929, so that he has
a fine record of public service behind him ... To fill the
office of Mayor during the year of the Coronation will be
a great honour not only for Mr Briggs but also for the
party he so ably represents. They have had to wait a long
time to see one of their number don the Mayoral robes."*

It was true, as it was said at the inauguration
ceremony:

*"Cambridge is a rather difficult place to serve as
Mayor. It is different altogether from many other towns,
because visitors come to it from across the seven seas to
conference meetings and it is the duty of the Mayor to
speak at gatherings on subjects about which he could
never have thought very much or of which he has small
knowledge."*

William himself was very aware of the privilege
that was his:

*"My feeling this morning is one of wonderment as to
what it is that controls some people's lives — what has
governed my life that I, out of a crowd of very ordinary
Cambridge people, should have been so guided that I
should become the chief citizen of a town of the renown
of Cambridge."*

There are hints here of a sense of the providence
of God guiding his life though it is not spelt out
explicitly.

Any misgivings that some in the City had at that
time were soon dispelled. William succeeded in the
role so well that he was called back to serve again
as Mayor in the difficult war years from 1943-44.
He received an OBE in 1941 for services to the town
in connection with his Civil Defence activities and

Lilian remembered him going to Buckingham Palace
to receive his award. It was said of him:

> *"Whether in the Council Chamber or on the Bench,
> he judged all things on their merits, and his ability to
> do this enabled him to be numbered among the most
> successful of Cambridge Mayors."*

One of his most treasured memories was the day
when he was invited to visit the Princes, George
and Edward, when they were up at college. This
took place sometime between October 1919 and
the summer of 1920 when the two brothers lived
in a private residence in Trumpington Road and
made their journeys into Trinity College on bicycles.

William talked to them about economics and surprised them by telling them that more money was being paid in dividends in the coal industry at that time than in wages. He was with them for about two hours.

Lilian reminisced with Frank about how she watched her father pass by in procession with Ramsey Macdonald who took over the leadership of the Labour Party from Keir Hardie in 1911. Hardie formed the first British Labour Government in 1924.

In addition to his many years of service within Cambridge City Council, court work also played a large part in Alderman Briggs' life. He was a magistrate for over thirty nine years and was Chairman of the Bench from 1945 until his retirement in 1951. He was the first Chairman of the Juvenile Court when it was instituted in 1933 and held the Chairmanship until 1948.

He died in 1957 aged eighty one and his funeral was a significant public occasion for the City. A civic procession was led by the mace bearer and an array of Councillors and Aldermen. They were followed by magistrates and judges, probation officers and representatives of the City Police Force. The Master of Pembroke College was present representing the University. This was the same man who had conferred on Alderman Briggs an honorary degree in 1951, on which occasion he had remarked:

"In the days of our forefathers, Town and Gown were in a state of perpetual feud. But that is a thing of the past, and among those responsible for our present mutual goodwill this man, too, should be numbered."

Professor Wade paid this tribute after those present at the City Petty Sessions had stood for a minute in silent tribute.

"All of us ... acknowledge the kindness he rendered to newcomers on the Bench ... It was a particular pleasure to me when, at the time of his retirement from the Bench, the University conferred on him the honorary degree of MA, not only for that service, but as a token of recognition for the many public services he rendered. He was a man of forthright character, transparent honesty and the highest integrity. But for these characteristics, he would not have accomplished what he did."

A representative of solicitors and barristers in the City revealed that many of them had first met him after returning from the Forces as young and inexperienced advocates. *"We could not have found a fairer or more impartial magistrate to deal with the business of the Court"*, he said. An inspector, speaking on behalf of Cambridge City Police, concluded his tribute by saying, *"He was a man of ordinary common-sense and I am sure it will be a long time before another man of his capabilities from his walk of life appears on the scene."* The reports of the funerals of both William and Elizabeth read like a 'Who's Who' of Cambridge society.

Mrs Briggs died in Addenbrookes Hospital just three years after her husband at the age of eighty three. There were also many fine tributes to her as she, too, had been very involved in service to the community and had been awarded the Service Medal and Certificate from the Soldiers, Sailors and Airmens Families Association. She was an ardent member of the Inner Wheel, an international women's organisation whose objectives are to promote true friendship, encourage the ideals of personal service, and to foster international understanding. She was particularly interested in the Coleridge School and did a great deal of voluntary work for Addenbrookes Hospital.

Her funeral service was also attended by many dignitaries, especially head-teachers and pupils from the Coleridge Schools for Boys and for Girls. I wondered whether Lilian and her sister had been pupils at the school.

These details may only be of passing interest to casual readers, but those who search wistfully in the hope of discovering something to celebrate in their family records will understand what it meant to Bev to read such glowing testimonials to his maternal Grandparents.

In the Cambridge archives, for the first time in his life, he found reasons to be proud of his heritage. Up to this point his perception of his natural family was mostly negative. There was no reason to think or speak of them; nothing to celebrate; nothing to pass on to our children and grandchildren that would help to build in them a sense of pride in their history and an appreciation of their place in the world. To discover these grandparents was an experience to treasure.

That evening we travelled out into a small country town in Cambridgeshire where Bev spoke to a fairly small group of Christian people and I found myself imagining how, many years before, grandfather Billie Briggs would have made similar journeys around the same area addressing such groups. Their messages were not the same, of course. Grandfather's socialism may have served the country well for a while, but the good news of Christ continues to change people the world over!

The next day we searched and found a small housing complex built in 1989 that had been named after him, 'Bill Briggs Court'. A resident was curious to see us taking photographs but when Bev started a conversation with him he wasn't much interested in the man whose name appeared over his home.

For the first time in his life, he found reasons to be proud of his heritage.

Just forty years after his death the community neither knew, nor seemed to care about what Billie had contributed to its wellbeing. We also visited the Council offices and photographed the plaque on which the list of Cambridge Mayors is recorded and sneaked into the Council Chamber to catch a glimpse of the place where Grandpa Briggs had once presided.

Chapter 25

POST PREGNANCY
- SEPTEMBER 2000

At the end of our week in and around Cambridge we returned the caravan to our friends in Oxfordshire and listened intently as Frank recounted details of his most recent visit to Lilian. He had found her looking well and happy and when he asked if she found his visits a strain she replied, *"Oh, no your visits aren't a strain, but seeing my husband and not telling him of our conversations about Beverley certainly is."*

She was interested in what we were doing that week and asked about our children and what they were like. She said several times how pleased she was that Beverley had turned out well. She commented that Teddy was *"a romancer with a gift with words"*.

She seemed to feel the need to talk about the circumstances surrounding Bev's birth and early years and Frank sensed again that it came as a great relief to her to talk about things of which she had never spoken in over fifty years.

Pregnancy, birth and cover up

She revealed that she had trained as a teacher at Homerton College in Cambridge, one of the best

Why would a mother leave her baby behind when she left the Nursing Home?

in the country at that time. She and Hector had started their married life in the city and she said that Michael had been born there although I had his birth certificate showing that he had actually been registered in Bristol. They moved to Winchester when Hector was promoted to be a Manager within the Liverpool Victoria Friendly Society. Ted Foderingham was on staff there when Hector arrived and he visited their home regularly. So the relationship between them developed and she became pregnant with Bev.

"Hector stood by me", she said. *"I can't speak too highly of him. He is such a good man. I couldn't possibly tell him about Beverley now."*

It seems that it was Hector who found the Nursing Home in the New Forest where she could give birth in complete privacy and he visited her there after the baby was born. When Frank asked how it was that Hector's name was on the birth certificate, she seemed surprised by the question. Why should it be otherwise? It was taken for granted that Hector would treat the child as if it were his own and so protect his wife's reputation.

But the deception fooled no one for long. Why would a mother leave her baby behind when she left the Nursing Home? That alone must have prompted questions among those who knew of her pregnancy and the staff who nursed her and her baby. She was a teacher who already had a healthy, happy four year old whom she obviously loved so why abandon this baby for months on end?

When it came to him being removed from the Nursing Home who took him away? Daisy Froud delivered him to the Savages but did she, a complete stranger, remove the child without the parents giving permission or being present?

And what of that name? *"So how did the baby*

come to be called Beverley?" Frank asked. *"Oh, Teddy just walked into the Nursing Home one day and said, "I have the name for him. Beverley.""* She didn't recall protesting or suggesting alternative names, she simply accepted what Ted said. The name Beverley, particularly at that time, would have been uncommon, especially for a boy. What was it that made him choose such a name for the boy? Could it have been the name of one of his family members?

> She last saw her child in a cot in the nursing home next to another baby who was deformed and also abandoned.

Reassurances and prevarication

After his birth Lilian continued to see Ted from time to time since she sometimes visited the office where he and her husband worked. When she asked Ted about the child's welfare he always reassured her that all was well with him and she need not worry on that account. Again she spoke of Michael being taken to visit the baby but he was too young to be aware of any relationship between them.

Frank sensed that she had some difficulty recalling the precise details. It had been a very traumatic time for her and, even though sixty years had passed since those events, her sense of guilt seemed to make the memories too painful to rehearse. She last saw her child in a cot in the nursing home next to another baby who was deformed and also abandoned.

She said that she had never expected that Teddy would adopt him since he was about to be called up for national service. But she did think that the Frouds would do so although nothing in their correspondence gives any clue to that ever being their intention. Daisy wrote in December 1950:

> *"Beverley came along and as far as we were told he was the offspring of a brother and that EC Foderingham was taking over the responsibility of keeping and educating him etc. and as we were sorry for the infant we agreed to*

help.

*When EC Foderingham was demobbed … we naturally
wanted to know about Beverley's future, for as you can
see, all our sympathy, generosity and care for Beverley
was thrown back at us and in fact, we were left with the
baby. We had only agreed to do what we could, providing
we had the help of ECF for we are elderly and could
not in any circumstances be expected to see the boy's
entry into manhood, for we should be too old to take
the responsibility of looking after such a young life and
furthermore, we think it wouldn't be fair to the boy or to
us."*

It seems that Lilian believed that the Frouds would
adopt him because that is what Ted wanted her to
think. Whether he really believed it himself must be
open to question for the reasons that Daisy states. It
seems much more likely that he was just hoping that
his generous friends, on whom he had come to rely,
would rescue him in some way from his dilemma.

In practice he appeared to ignore the problem
hoping that it would simply go away. He could
hardly have expected that it would take ten troubled
years before he could be rid of the child. How much
better it would have been for everyone involved if
Ted had faced up to his responsibilities and made
proper arrangements for the child to be adopted
by a couple who really wanted him rather than
being fought over by people who came to resent his
presence. However, if that had happened Bev's life
might well have turned out to be very different to
what it was with no guarantee that he would have
fared better than he did.

Lilian was probably unaware of all this until she
was contacted ten years after his birth. She told
Frank that she remembered receiving a telegram
from the Frouds asking her to go at once to sign

some papers, presumably the forms that gave permission for Bev to be admitted to The Childrens' Home & Mission (Mill Grove). The urgency of the situation arose from Daisy's advanced illness and imminent death and Lilian responded immediately.

A new start – but memories lingered on

It transpired that a year after Bev's birth, Hector moved his family from Winchester to Andover, 15 miles away, no doubt in an effort to put the unpleasantness of the previous two years behind them, and in doing so he accepted demotion. As Lilian said, "This was typical of him. He did it because of me." Michael was five and their baby daughter just a few months old when they moved and so living in a different community, in another home and with Lilian's arms filled again with a baby, Hector hoped that Ted Foderingham and his influence would soon became just a memory. But Lilian could not forget her lover. In 1986 she had seen the notice of his death published in the local press and had presumed that he died in Bishopstoke. She knew little else about him except that she had heard that he had four children. Indeed he had, but one, her son, he never did acknowledge as his own.

SOMEBODY'S SON

Chapter 26

A SEAMAN FROM BARBADOS
- SEPTEMBER 2000

We found information from the Southampton Archives Service waiting for us when we arrived home from our tour of East Anglia. It included photocopies of the identification cards for both Merchant Seamen, Edward Foderingham, Ted's father, and of Leslie Haines Foderingham, possibly his brother. The photograph on the reverse side of Edward's card showed him to be unmistakably West Indian. In that moment, as we stared at it, all the fanciful conjectures that had filled the vacuum of our ignorance ended decisively.

The discovery of Grandfather Briggs' outstanding public service in Cambridge left us on a high. Standing in our lounge just a few days later staring at Grandfather Foderingham had a quite different and profound effect. I handed the cards to Bev and he stood silently studying the face of his grandfather for some time, not so much searching for recognition, I think, but wrestling with his first emotional response to the unequivocal confirmation of his paternal black West Indian ancestry. The revelation stopped him in his tracks and threw him into turmoil.

Every stain of racism and xenophobia had long since been expunged from us, or so we thought, when for ten years we lived in Willesden, North West London, with its colourful cosmopolitan community. There we rubbed shoulders every day with our neighbours who came from many different parts of the globe including the West Indies, Africa and Asia. We also had a large Jewish community nearby and our own children could name several nationalities among their close friends. We regarded that as a very good thing.

One warm summer Sunday afternoon, we stood in our back garden and listed the sounds that bombarded our ears. The siren of a fire engine sounded as it left the fire station a few hundred yards away. Sounds from the hospital opposite mingled with the voices of our Jewish neighbours in the maisonette above who, with windows wide open, practised a Gilbert and Sullivan operetta.

In the park behind us an Irish festival, with its amplified accordion and violin accompaniment, was in full swing and at the park gate a West Indian lady speaker was using her loud hailer to great effect as with immense enthusiasm she regaled everyone within a hundred yards of her preaching. Over the fence our Polish neighbours were entertaining their friends, laughing and playing with the children.

And above the cacophony, almost noiselessly, a new Boeing 747 lifted gracefully into the sky over our heads heading out of London Heathrow.

With that experience behind us, why was Bev's reaction to the photograph so strong? Let him try to explain:

Meeting Grandfather Briggs gave me reasons to think that I really belonged by birth-right to a family to be proud of, an English family from a prestigious city. For a few days I had begun to feel differently about myself. I was someone after all. I belonged to a blood line that connected me to a notable ancestor. Then this!

Cambridge had told only half a story. In truth I'm not a white Englishman alone. I'm of mixed race, neither one thing nor another.

The revelation was not entirely unexpected but when it came it was sudden, stark, conclusive. Our family habit of a relaxed, even humorous, reference to mysterious colour from unknown relatives vanished instantly. Now a black merchant seaman stared back at me from the page, equally my grandfather.

In denial

But who is he? Where did he come from? Is he a man to be proud of? Will I ever want to talk about him? No! Let's keep this quiet. Let's put all the pieces of my life back in the box where they belong and close the lid and lock it for ever. All my life I had passed as a white Englishman with just a hint of dark skin so let's continue as though nothing has changed. "Look at our blond blue-eyed daughter", I'll say. "The very image of an English rose."

Maybe this is what I had feared all along, that

> I wished passionately that it didn't matter, but in that moment it felt as though it mattered very much.

we would get so far in our search only for it to end in discoveries that would threaten and change us forever.

I was no more black the day after I had seen that photograph than I had been all my life and yet I felt that blackness was no longer out there in other people with whom I lived happily, it was in here, in me, it ran in my veins and showed in my skin.

My first instinct was to run from it, frightened by it, more to the point, by what it might mean in my relationships with other people. A secret with which I had flirted all my life suddenly became a present and unwelcome reality.

I was known as a leader by a few thousand people throughout the UK. How will they react when they learn the truth about me? Conversations in which good friends had expressed their racial prejudices when they thought it safe to do so came back to remind me that, whatever we may like to portray, prejudice is never far away. Perhaps it would be best if I quietly withdrew from them and from public life so that they would not be embarrassed by discovering my identity and I would not be hurt if they chose to regard me differently.

Then guilt

But soon guilt set in. Something happened in that moment standing in our lounge. I had discovered a terrible truth about myself. I was no more than a racist at heart, too ashamed and distressed to confront the truth that I am both white and black. I wished passionately that it didn't matter, but in that moment it felt as though it mattered very much.

Today there are over 1.2 million people of mixed race living in the UK alone. It is the fastest growing minority group in the country, but back in the 1940's mixed race marriages, and children of mixed parentage were despised. They emerged from docklands and from military towns where frustrated sailors and soldiers made love as they passed through. Society regarded them as shameful and their children as, at the very least, unfortunates.

Now as I write, seventeen years on from the day when I first saw the image of Grandfather Foderingham, I can see how irrational and disproportionate my reactions were, but they were painfully real at the time. Now the story is here for all to read and I am pleased to tell it at last. I have had a growing appreciation over the intervening years of the positive value of having a direct blood line to the two thirds world. The genes of former slaves are in my DNA and I'm proud of that especially because, at the heart of Christianity is the message that God favours the poor, the disenfranchised and disadvantaged.

"Think of what you were when you were called. Not many of you were wise by human standards; not many were influential; not many of you were of noble birth. But God chose the foolish things of this world to shame the wise; God chose the weak things of the world to shame the strong. He chose the lowly things of this world and the despised things – and the things that are not – to nullify the things that are, so that no one may boast before Him."*

When Christ walked the earth the nation with which he identified most closely had at one time emerged from slavery and the people who responded first to his teaching, and became his disciples, were those who had little status in this world. Like Archbishop Justin Welby, I have experienced deeply and personally the liberating truth that deals with the pain of human disfunctionality and differences of race, colour and social status. *I know that I find who I am in*

> The genes of former slaves are in my DNA and I'm proud of that.

*1 Cor 1:26

Lost between the worlds.

Jesus Christ, not in genetics. My identity in Him never changes."

Would other people react in the same way?

Occasionally I have wondered how a Barbadian, or any other person of African descent, might react if they found out later in life that they had white ancestry? Would they have similar feelings to mine? I thought that they might but decided to ask some African friends to imagine, if they could, how they would feel in such a situation.

Two black African doctors explained that within their culture the hardest thing to deal with would be to discover that they had ancestry linking them to another tribe, especially one that was regarded as inferior to theirs. White ancestry on the other hand is generally regarded as a positive thing in their society as long as it comes from reputable people.

When I asked the question of a West Indian friend she surprised me by revealing that she had a mix of both Dutch and Italian ancestry. She had known about that all her life and had hated her brother for being whiter than she is.

She explained that discovering a white connection later in life wouldn't have the same effect on all West Indians. For many, white people remind them of slavery, inequality and prejudice which still excludes them from many advantages. Mixed race Trinidadians, for example, can find themselves ostracised and bullied by both white and black communities, lost between the worlds. So discovering one's mixed ancestry later in life could cause many to experience very similar feelings to those that ambushed me that day.

I found comfort in those conversations. Maybe I was not the racist that I had at first thought but I simply needed time to come to terms with the revelation and negotiate my way through the implications of it for me personally, for us as a family and for our wider circle of friends and acquaintances."

Chapter 27
MORE REVELATIONS - OCTOBER 2000

Even though it had been three weeks since Frank's last visit, Lilian was ready when he arrived and was clearly expecting him. She seemed less confused this time, although recalling dates and times remained challenging. "She looked as though she had aged," Frank reported, "Older but in good health – and she had her glasses on this time."

The reason for this last comment was that we had collected some photographs for him to show her and he had asked her to have her glasses with her so that she could see them. The photos included some of the recent wedding of our son, Ian, and one which showed our three adult children with their spouses and our first three grandchildren, her great-grandchildren. She was thrilled to see them and commented again on how much Bev looked like his father.

She gave particular attention to Philip, our eldest son, seeing some resemblance between him and Ted Foderingham. When she saw the photograph of our grandson, Christopher, with his auburn hair she immediately opened her diary from which she produced a similar snapshot of one of her great grandchildren. Frank looked at them side by side and described them as looking like 'two peas in a pod'.

Lilian was particularly fascinated by the pictures we had taken in Cambridge. "Oh, that's the house where I was born. However did they know that?" she remarked. She seemed delighted that we had gone to so much trouble to trace her background and recognised at once the newspaper photographs of her father's Mayoral inauguration and one published at the time of their Golden wedding anniversary. "I've got that photo at home!" she said with excitement, obviously pleased that we appeared to be as proud of her father as she was.

She was quite confused about the dates of her teacher training and vague about the date of her marriage but she gave Frank the impression that she went straight from school to college around 1929 after which she then worked for a while at St Philip's School in Cambridge. She seemed surer about the fact that she and Hector married at St Philip's church in Mill Road, the church they and her parents had attended for some years.

She recalled that it was through her father's influence that Hector obtained employment with Liverpool and Victoria and she was quite clear about their subsequent move to Bristol where Michael was born. This confirmed what I had found in the records.

She described Hector as being a very capable worker with much promise and this was confirmed by the fact that he was promoted to manage the Winchester office. It was then that they moved to the village of Allbrook, south of Winchester, and her relationship with Ted began.

Separation and reconciliation

As she opened her heart to Frank it became clear that her relationship with Ted went well beyond what we had previously imagined. She revealed that she actually moved out of the family home, taking three year old Michael with her, and went to live in a flat that Ted had rented in Southampton. It was there that Bev was conceived in December 1939.

It was also news to us that Lilian's father had become aware of her pregnancy from quite early on. We had wondered whether he ever knew of Bev's existence or whether it had been hidden from him. The irony was not lost on us that he who was a magistrate in Cambridge for nearly forty years and the first Chairman of the Juvenile Court who presided over hundreds of cases related to the welfare of children, had no input at all into the life of his own grandson. Lilian's only comment was, "He was sorry about my behaviour, but he never blamed me." Frank gathered from that that her father thought her actions unfortunate, but he didn't try to persuade her to return to Hector.

Hector emerges as a courageous man who knew his own mind and who would not give up on his wife. He continued to contact her and to plead with her until he succeeded in convincing her of his love and forgiveness and of his determination to win her back. "It was just like him to do that," Lilian said. So we gathered that she returned to him sometime before Bev's birth in August the following year and just two months later their daughter was conceived.

Lilian talked of her visits to Bev in the Nursing Home, taking baby clothes with her which she had knitted for him because the nurses said he was cold. At various points during the conversation she was in tears, tears of joy more than of sorrow, but tears of frustration as well.

> The first Chairman of the Juvenile Court had no input at all into the life of his own grandson.

Searching for a way forward

Several times she expressed the dilemma she felt in wanting to see Bev but not at the expense of deceiving Hector. Sometimes she said that she would tell him, and then she would feel that she couldn't. She said that she couldn't tell her daughter because she knew nothing of Bev's existence and would be devastated. Frank ventured the thought that her daughter might be glad to know that she had a brother, and to know of his family too, but Lilian did not reply.

I had a recording of Bev preaching at a recent Harvest Service and suggested to Frank that she might like to hear it, but it was not to be. Lilian warmed to the idea but was not prepared to go through with it without Hector's knowledge. Frank suggested that she might tell Hector that it was Bev who had traced her, that this was in no way her initiative. He offered to explain the situation personally to Hector, an idea that appealed to her, but on second thoughts she said that she felt that she should be the first one to explain matters.

Noticing that the conversation was beginning to become stressful for her, Frank prepared to leave. As he did so he offered to visit her again in three weeks or maybe, if it was too much for her, he would leave it longer. She asked him to come in three weeks and said that she would ask Mrs Heron to get in touch with him if she made any decisions in the meantime, or if there were any other developments.

Hector and Lilian were married in Cambridge in 1933 so, at the time of Frank's visits, they had been together for a remarkable sixty seven years. No wonder that she felt unable to take any action without his knowledge. To her it felt deceitful, doing something behind the back of the man who had a deep lifelong love for her.

Their marriage had survived her love affair sixty years earlier and together they had provided a stable and loving home for their two children. She had served hundreds of children and their families as Headmistress of the school in Tidworth and had gone on in retirement to make a significant contribution to the community in which they lived.

The siblings' education

All the children born into the Foderingham and Fletcher families had a privileged education. All three of the Foderingham children were privately educated and as for the Fletchers, Michael was privately educated and, with Lilian being a Head Teacher, he and his sister were both given all the support they could have wished for during their early years.

This was not so for Bev, of course, who as predicted, found theological college a considerable challenge. His course required him to learn both Hebrew and Greek when he had but a tentative grasp of English grammar. He did, however, complete the college course successfully, gaining a distinction in Systematic Theology and has sustained a public preaching and teaching ministry for over 50 years, addressing audiences in many parts of the UK and elsewhere in the world.

His ability to communicate was never in doubt but few will know what a lifetime of reading and study has cost him so that he could complete the task to which he knew he had been called from his early 'teens. Edwin's prayers came true, "… *and we all pray that … in the end Beverley will be an outstanding active and forceful 'messenger'.*"

Before leaving, Frank told Mrs Heron about the photographs that he had shown Lilian and of her emotional response to them and suggested that she might be glad of some support that afternoon. They also discussed her struggle as she thought about whether or not to reveal to Hector our contact with her. Apparently Hector and Lilian sometimes had an hour alone together each week before members of the family returned to take him home. That could provided her with an opportunity to tell him if she ever felt able to do so.

Chapter 28
LONG-REMEMBERED PLACES
- OCTOBER 2000

B
ev had a weekend free, the last one in the year
2000, so we decided to use it to press on with
our research. The whole project was proving a
distraction and had become very unsettling for him,
so I felt that we needed to bring it to some kind of
conclusion as soon as we could.

I realized now that, when I began my project, I
was under the illusion that discovering the facts,
compiling a family tree and writing up the record of
Bev's life, would be sufficient to satisfy our curiosity
and lead to a settled and happy conclusion. It proved
to be far more intense and disturbing than that and
I was left wondering what it would take to bring
closure. Perhaps nothing short of a meeting with
one or other of his natural relatives would do that
but, given the circumstances, that seemed a remote
possibility.

Grandmother Kate Goodwin
I had sent again to Southampton Registry Office for
Grandmother Kate's birth certificate rather assuming
that she had been born in that area but there was
no trace of her. So again we visited the Winchester
Records Office and searched through the micro-fiche

> Marrying a black man would most likely have scandalised the rural community in which she was raised, if not her own family

films for any trace of her.

From Ted's birth certificate I already knew that her maiden name was Goodwin and I also discovered that she had died in 1921 at the age of thirty eight. It took some time, but eventually we found her, Kate May Goodwin, born in Witney, Oxfordshire, in 1883 sometime between April and June and married to Edward twenty years later in Southampton. It was understandable that she married in Southampton rather than in Witney since marrying a black man would most likely have scandalised the rural community in which she was raised, if not her own family.

From Winchester we drove the fifteen miles to Southampton and along Millbrook Road where she had once lived, searching for clues to point us in the direction of York Terrace where she gave birth to Ted, Bev's father, in January 1906, but we were to be frustrated for where the house once stood there was a busy dual carriageway.

However, we did note a boarded up pub called 'The Sailor's Rest' and at the sight of it my imagination began to run riot. Perhaps young Kate worked there as a barmaid and first met the handsome 28 year old West Indian seaman when he came in for a pint.

Visual memory triggers

Over the years we had returned to the area many times but we had never previously sought out the places where Bev had lived during his early childhood. So, since we had some time to spare, I suggested that we left Southampton and made our way to Chandlers Ford where he lived long ago in a bungalow. I hoped to build up a visual image of the places where the drama of his early years had been played out and I also wondered if a return to

Chandlers Ford might trigger memories in him that still lay hidden. It was, after all, his return to Tiptree that had first awakened his interest in his past so perhaps that would happen again.

And sure enough, as we searched out the two schools that he attended, more memories were stirred and some incidents, of which he had never spoken, took shape in his mind.

It took us a little while to find his Infants School. As a child he had often been too unwell to attend but he had a clear picture of where it was located. "Yes, that's it. There were some huts at the back somewhere. Yes! Look there are still some there, looking just about the same as I remember them. The headmaster was a Mr Mann. There used to be a school gate there which I ran into and cracked my head open. The school bus stopped at the bottom of the road. One morning I ran out from behind it into the path of a car and was knocked down and the police were called. There was a bridge just down there somewhere where I hid the bike."

From the school we went back through Chandlers Ford to Leigh Road where the bungalow stood. It was no longer the well-appointed extensive property it had once been for, where just one bungalow with its separate garage had once stood, there were now two.

As we studied it through the car window he described in detail the layout of the old place, even recalling the distinctively fishy smell that he associated with the kitchen, and for the first time he mentioned the quarrels between Marjorie and Daisy. I had always imagined that he must have been within earshot of them but he had never spoken of them previously.

I asked, "Did the two women share the same kitchen?" The question caught him by surprise and he thought for a while before answering. "I don't remember Daisy Froud ever cooking at all; she was probably too ill to cope with that. But we didn't eat with the Foderinghams either since we lived separate lives. Oh, yes! I do remember now walking up the road to a cafe on the corner with Bournemouth Road and carrying back plates with our meals on them."

This immediately struck me as a somewhat hazardous task to give to an eight or nine year old, especially a youngster who had a reputation for rushing around and being accident prone. But who else was available to cook for him and Daisy during school holidays or when Edwin was at work?

Another memory was triggered as we sat there of how he would quietly let himself out into the garden when Daisy was asleep and crawl under the fence to spend time with a kind old lady next door who sat him down in her small lean-to conservatory and gave him things to eat and drink as they talked together. What stories he told her of life in the bungalow, or fantasy tales he regaled her with is anyone's guess.

We took a photograph of the bungalow and drove on to find an address in the village of Allbrook some five miles away that was new to us both. I had noted it on Bev's birth certificate. It had been Lilian and Hector Fletcher's home in 1940. It proved to be a disappointing, rundown, nondescript semidetached house built in the typical style of the nineteen thirties. We slowed only slightly as we drove past and didn't take a photograph. I remember saying, "It doesn't look much, does it? But that place must have witnessed so much passion and pain when Hector and Lilian lived there."

From there we went to find the last location of the day, a Club in Eastleigh where Bev's half-brother was the manager. It had occurred to me that we might be able to wander in as customers and meet him casually if the opportunity arose but as it turned out the Club was closed and the evening session was reserved for club members only so we never did meet him.

We spent a restless night in a busy, noisy hotel in Southampton, our minds working over the events of the day. The next morning over breakfast I told Bev that I had begun to consider writing to Marjorie Foderingham directly, appealing to her to give us further information and perhaps some photographs of the family. To my surprise he didn't immediately discount the idea and as we left for home we continued to discuss the implications.

A detour
We had travelled just twenty miles when on an impulse we decided to take a detour to Tidworth where Lilian had been the Headmistress of a school for over 20 years.

Earlier telephone enquiries to the library there, and correspondence with a Records office in Trowbridge, had left unresolved the question of exactly which school she led, the Church of England school within the Army Garrison or the now demolished school that had once stood in Station Road.

We found the Army Garrison and gingerly approached the gate. The soldiers on duty there soon made it obvious that our request to view the school was unscheduled and needed special permission. Our story must have sounded rather feeble to them and the fact that we were carrying a camera did not help. However, we were reluctantly directed to the guardroom and, after searching the car, an officer provided us with a pass and a young military escort to direct us to what had once been the Garrison Infants and Junior School.

It was a sorry sight, closed and looking rather

derelict. However, as a listed building we were told its future was assured. Although we weren't allowed inside, we did our best to take as many photographs as we could from various angles around the building unsure that we were capturing the features that would best serve to stimulate Lilian's memory of her years there.

Having been escorted back to the Garrison gate and seen off the premises, we made our way to a new Leisure Centre in the village hoping to find the Library within the complex.

Someone who knew everyone

We expected it to be closed on a Sunday so we simply planned to note its location and opening times to visit it on another occasion. However, an unexpected conversation with a member of staff behind the enquiry desk of the Leisure Centre proved to be really helpful. When I explained why we were there, she told me about the school she had attended in the village and, although I quickly realised that she would have been far too young to have known Lilian, she went on to tell me that her mother had lived in Tidworth all her life and had worked in the Post Office. She knew just about everyone in the village and, what is more, she was very interested in researching family history having looked into her own family background extensively.

This was just the kind of contact I needed. If anyone could remember Lilian it would be this lady. Even if she had not met her personally she might well be able to give me some impressions of her from the people who had known her, pupils or maybe teachers who had worked with her. I took her details and we left for home having gathered more information than we could possibly have hoped for.

Chapter 29
MARJORIE - OCTOBER 2000

Next day I wasted no time in preparing a letter to Marjorie. It read as follows;

Dear Mrs. Foderingham,

You will, I'm sure, be surprised to receive this letter. My name is Valerie Savage and in recent months I have been doing some research into my husband's family background.

Although he was born some time before you met your husband you will presumably remember Beverley. Last year Mrs. Savage died and so we feel that we are freer to make our enquiries. We had never wanted to cause pain to his adoptive parents. They were very good to him and did provide at least some stability for him during a disturbed childhood. We now have three adult married children and four grandchildren and I am sure that you as a mother, and perhaps a grandmother, will understand that we feel we owe it to our children to give them some sense of their roots and background.

Bev has never been a person who looks back. He certainly does not express any bitterness about the circumstances of his childhood and we understand that it was a very difficult and painful situation for everyone concerned at the time. Mrs. Foderingham, we really do not want to cause you any distress but you are perhaps the only person who can help us. We have thought very carefully before approaching you and we hope that this will be just one single request of you.

All that we are asking for is some information and we would very much appreciate some photographs. We would like to know about Mr. Foderingham's family. Can you tell us anything about them at all? Do you have any photos of his parents or of any brothers and sisters? Our research so far indicates some connection with Barbados in the West Indies. Do you know of any living relatives out there? We would be interested to know how your children have gone on in life. We understand that your son is manager of the very successful Club in Southampton. We will gladly return anything you send to us once we have seen it.

We do hope that you will not easily dismiss this letter. We feel that this could perhaps help us to draw a line under the past after all this time.

You may be interested to know that Beverley did theological training in South Wales and after that ministered in two churches in London. He is now the General Secretary of a group of churches across the whole country. He travels extensively acting as a consultant to these many churches. I'm sure you will be glad that things have worked for good in our lives.

We look forward to hearing from you.
Valerie Savage

I posted it with some nervousness on Monday October 23rd. Three days later I received a telephone call from her.

I had imagined that Marjorie would be a mellow old lady who, like Lilian, would be glad of an opportunity to make her peace for past wrongs, perhaps extend a hand of friendship and show her understanding, but it was not to be. She was not directly hostile, but from the beginning of our conversation she was self-justifying and defensive.

She began by saying that my letter had been a shock to her and she was very sorry but she would not be able to help us at all since she had no photographs and knew nothing about her husband's family.

After her initial brittleness she calmed a little as I kept her talking. She began to explain to me how she came to Chandlers Ford as an immature twenty-one year old and had endured seven years of absolute misery there. She had been told many untruths but, being so young and inexperienced and imagining herself in love, she had believed what she had been told. Ted lied to her about his age, pretending to be younger than he was. In 1945 he was thirty nine and she twenty one, a difference of eighteen years.

She said that her family in Wales was very uncertain about her relationship with Ted. Her brother was particularly uneasy, warning the family that, being wartime, there were many men away from home who weren't at all what they seemed to be.

> Being wartime, there were many men away from home who weren't at all what they seemed to be.

But she and her family had been reassured when Ted took Daisy Froud to Wales to meet them, passing her off as his sister. How he managed to do this immediately struck me as odd since Daisy would have been fifty three when Ted and Marjorie married. It seemed scarcely believable that Daisy would go along with this deception and that Edwin would know nothing of it. Anyway, it directly contradicted the Frouds' account that they knew nothing of the wedding until two years after it had happened.

She claimed to have been born the daughter of a vicar in Pembrokeshire, which she was quick to point out is known as 'Little England'. They were married in Llanelly and their wedding was a huge affair conducted by an Archdeacon or some other elevated church dignitary; a relative she said.

Coming from such a privileged background it came as a terrible shock to her to live in "that awful bungalow with those wicked people". When I ventured to suggest that it was a very difficult situation for everyone who lived there, she insisted that it was far worse for her since she was so young.

She was right, of course, but she seemed not to have considered what it had been like for the five, six, seven year old boy who was caught in the cross fire of warring adults, although she did add, "It was a poor little life for Beverley. He should never have been there with that old woman".

Marjorie attributed all the problems entirely to Daisy. Ted had lived with her and Edwin for a long time before she knew him and, "Daisy was possessive over him". This confirmed my suspicion that Daisy had wanted to have Bev there with her as a way of keeping a hold over Ted.

Distressing revelations

It was not until after their marriage that Marjorie was told by others that Ted's father was from the West Indies and was black. When she heard that, she was extremely upset and tried to hide it from relatives who were staying with them at the time. She also discovered from a doctor friend that it was commonly believed that Bev was Ted's son but then she made a point of mentioning that Hector Fletcher was named on Beverley's birth certificate as his father, not Ted. So she had checked his birth certificate then, and had confirmed for herself that there was no proof that he was a Foderingham, even if she knew that to be true.

At her insistence, Marjorie had eventually been introduced to Ted's family but the meeting did not go well and they never saw each other again, or so she claimed.

I asked if Ted's mother was English and she answered that she had come from somewhere near Aylesbury and had moved to Southampton. When I mentioned that I thought his mother had died young she confirmed this to be true. She had died on her way to hospital where she was about to give birth to twins, both of whom must have died with her since there is no record of any Foderingham births in 1921.

She spoke of the wickedness of the Frouds in sending her anonymous letters. This was the first time that we had heard of such a thing. Apparently the police were informed and, although nothing was proved, they were of the opinion that Daisy Froud had coerced Edwin into writing them. Anonymous letters had also been sent to her family in Wales, the final one arrived following Daisy's death.

Marjorie strongly advised me to tell Bev not to press on any further to enquire into the Foderingham family. She had not been at all impressed with them, though they thought Ted had done well for himself. "Even though I say so myself, I was very attractive", she said.

> **Even though I say so myself, I was very attractive**

While she freely admitted that Ted had told her 'stories' which had trapped her for seven years in a dire situation, she insisted that, "It did not cause any trouble between us. We went on to be a very happy, close little family and, when Ted died, the church was packed for his funeral."

At the mention of his name I asked if she could supply Bev with a photograph of him since he had none. This was clearly a step too far. She simply stated that she had none having given them all to her family – a disappointing response, impossible to believe.

Following our telephone conversation my curiosity

got the better of me. If, as she had said, there had been such a grand wedding and her family were so well known in church circles, then there was the distinct possibility that there would be mention of it at the time in the local newspaper accompanied, perhaps, by a photograph. To find any press record of the wedding I would need to know the exact date it took place so I sent to Llanelly for a copy of Ted and Marjorie's marriage certificate.

When it arrived I quickly scanned its details. Yes, Marjorie was just twenty years old on November 13th 1943 when they married and he was thirty seven. But her father, William Badham, is recorded as being a blacksmith not a minister and the wedding was conducted by a D. M. Jones, Vicar. Her address is given as being in Llanelly, Carmarthenshire, although she may well have been born in 'Little England' as she claimed. Ted is recorded as the only son of the late Honourable and Mrs E Foderingham, a title that had no foundation in fact as far as I can tell, and he was certainly not the 'only child' as I was later to discover.

On a later visit to Llanelly we found, as we were led to expect, a report of the wedding in The Llanelly & County Guardian for November 18th 1943. It read, "There was a large attendance of guests and well-wishers. The Venerable D. Morgan Jones BA., assisted by the Rev D. Reece, MA, and the Rev D. Islwyn Lewis officiated, and Mr D. J. Evans was the organist, the service being fully choral. … the newly wedded couple left for London en route to Bournemouth, where the honeymoon is being spent." So Marjorie did have a memorable wedding day as she claimed, over which notable church dignitaries officiated – and Ted had made an impression as he usually did.

Foderingham grandparents

Despite Marjorie's warnings, or maybe because
of them, I was keen to find out more about the
Foderingham family focusing now on Kate and
Edward, Bev's paternal grandparents. Marjorie had
said she knew nothing of them but in fact she had
inadvertently told me things that I had not known
previously and that made me even more curious.

Kate's death certificate confirmed that she was
seven months pregnant when she went into a
nephritic coma and died on September 16th in
1921 in Havelock Road. She was thirty eight. The
mysterious letters 'UD' on the certificate, might
indicate that she was actually in transit at the time
of her death as Marjorie had said. Her death was
registered by her sister who was present.

[I have a slight and completely illogical fear as I
write this since our daughter, Kate, is just now seven
months pregnant.]

Kate and Edward's marriage took place on
September 12th 1903 in the Parish Church of
Freemantle, also an area of Southampton. Edward
was twenty seven and Kate twenty. He is recorded
as being a mariner but she apparently had no
profession. Their two sons, Edward (Ted) Bev's
father, and Leslie seemed to have inherited more of
their mother's genes than their father's. Few seem
to have noticed Ted's mixed ethnicity and Leslie is
described on his seaman's identity card as being 5'8"
tall with fair hair and complexion and blue eyes.

Chapter 30

SHE WANTS TO SEE YOU - NOVEMBER 2000

It had been several weeks since Frank's last visit to Lilian. Since he had heard nothing from her during that time, we assumed that she was still considering if she should speak to Hector or to her daughter about us.

As time passed we were finding it more difficult to live with her indecision. Frank's first contact with her had been in the middle of August and, although many good things had resulted from his mediation, a momentum had been created by the success of my research that had led to an increased longing for Bev to establish a direct personal relationship with his mother before it was too late.

We understood her dilemma, of course, and sympathised with it very much and worried that she might find it all too much and become ill. However, from what Frank said, she generally seemed to be enjoying the experience.

For all my expanding files of information, we still had no idea of what Lilian looked like or sounded like, we had only Frank's reports. We knew, of course, that she was very elderly and had understandable lapses of memory but does she have a sense of humour? She obviously has a

> **Had we really come this far only to be frustrated in the end?**

twinkle in her eye from time to time but is she a very serious person? Is her voice refined or does it have a distinctive accent? Was she a strict parent, a bossy headmistress or somewhat more relaxed in her leadership of others? We simply did not know.

Maybe after all Bev will have to be content with finding and meeting her daughter, his half-sister but that could be some time away when both Hector and Lilian have passed on.

But, inconvenient as it was, we had uncovered deeply buried, unresolved issues that Bev had carried all his life and, since the opportunity allowed it, a face to face meeting with his mother could prove to be hugely significant in him coming to terms with his past. Had we really come this far only to be frustrated in the end? Maybe Frank's next visit to her could bring some resolution to the dilemmas we were all now facing.

Frank's report

He came to our home with his wife, Betty, immediately following his fifth visit to the nursing home. He clearly enjoyed his visits and, having long since overcome his initial anxieties, found it stimulating to work with us on this very personal project. His first words to us were, "She's a lovely lass this mother of yours". He spoke again of her warmth and friendliness and said that he had three main areas that he wanted to talk to us about.

Firstly, more information had emerged about Hector. He had been in the Air Force during the war working as an armourer when one day, when he had been loading a bomb, it exploded and he lost his hand. Later a second operation became necessary when a part of his arm also had to be removed but despite his disability, Hector, a very good pianist, continued to play with one hand and he had learned to manage day to day tasks very well.

The second area that Frank and Lilian had talked of concerned her relationship with Ted. She confided that their relationship had lingered on for some time even after she had returned home to Hector. She remembered that she and Hector were away together at a holiday camp one time and Ted rented a house nearby so they could meet clandestinely. They clearly had difficulty in making a complete break from each other.

❝❝And finally ... she wants to see you!"

"And finally ...!" Frank came to his last point with obvious relish. It was clearly to be the climax of his report. "And finally ... she wants to see you!" Really? Could it really be true? These were words we had been aching to hear and doubting if they would ever come.

Frank went on, "Yes. She has come to the decision that she will see Bev but she will not tell Hector."

It is just what we had begun to hope would happen, and thankfully she had reached this decision without any pressure from us. Frank had been keeping this good news until last for, as he had said to Betty on the way to us, "If I tell him that first, he won't hear anything else I say", which was almost certainly true.

Frank had made provisional plans for our visit and it was not long after they left that Bev was on the phone to confirm arrangements with Mrs Heron. Lilian was due to go on a rare outing from the Home to a hospital appointment that week so we arranged to see her the following week. Bev had only the Wednesday morning available when it just so happened that we were due to travel to Bournemouth, a journey that took us very close to Andover and the nursing home where Lilian was a resident.

For all that it seemed to take so long to meet

Lilian, when we looked back on it later we were relieved and very grateful that we had reached such a positive conclusion. Frank, with his relaxed and gentle manner and genuine interest in people, proved to be just the right person to act as our intermediary. As an older man, he won Lilian's confidence and she came to trust him and confide in him freely.

It also seemed to us quite remarkable that, although she had attended Anglican churches all her life, she had been prepared to receive a Baptist Minister as she had already attended a Baptist Chapel. Frank was able to give to Lilian, and to her son, just the practical and spiritual support they needed during what was a disturbing journey for them both.

Chapter 31

THE REVEAL
- NOVEMBER 2000

When Bev's reactions to meeting Grandfather Foderingham had settled, we began to consider when and how we would tell our children and their spouses about our discovery. It would be impossible to keep it to ourselves since they knew about my research and would almost certainly ask about any new developments when an opportunity presented itself.

We were particularly anxious about what effect the news would have on Ian, our second son, with his slightly darker skin colouring. If Bev had been so affected by the experience, how might he respond? We enlarged the small photograph on the card from the archive and Edward appeared as a handsome man with the tight crinkly hair and the typical features of his race.

Bev was preaching at The Slade in South East London and, since it was only just over thirty miles from where Ian and Suzie, our daughter-in-law lived, we took the opportunity to spend some time with them. Although Kate also lived in the area, we decided not to talk to her yet as she was seven months pregnant with her second child, exactly the time when her Great Grandmother, also Kate, had died.

Looking into this stranger's eyes felt like meeting someone familiar.

Moving through the story, watching their reactions
Although we attempted to lighten the atmosphere when we met, the truth was that we had never before had a serious conversation with our son about his colouring. Why would we? He was always just our boy who we loved and of whom we were very proud. It's true, we had wondered from time to time if there had ever been speculation about his background or whether this had been a source of embarrassment to him, but nothing more.

So little by little we told them the story of our search, the people we had met and the places we had visited, trying to avoid too much detail and stopping from time to time to explain some of the more complicated parts. It was a lot for them to absorb in one sitting.

Ever practical, Ian eventually interrupted us asking us to draw a family tree so that he could fathom the complicated relationships that we had been outlining.

Then we produced the photograph of Grandfather Edward Foderingham watching them closely for any signs that they were embarrassed or upset, but they were clearly fascinated. They began to speculate that he also may have been of mixed race as he did not appear to them to be very dark. Suzie stared at the photograph on her own for some time and eventually remarked that, looking into this stranger's eyes felt like meeting someone familiar, meaning we presumed that she could see Ian's eyes looking back at her. It was not so much the colour but the set and shape of those eyes that had a familiarity about them.

They were both absorbed by what we had to say and seemed to treat each revelation as just another fact to take on board. They showed no emotion and this was a relief to us since we could only guess at how they would react.

Suzie might have become distressed or have felt that she had entered into marriage unfairly disadvantaged by our ignorance of the past and unprepared for what might happen when she became a mother. Ian was a little more predictable since, whatever his true feelings, he has always been embarrassed by any show of emotion and reticent about sharing any feelings of his own.

From the few comments he made at the end of our discussion, I was surprised to find out that he remembered how, years previously, he had asked Bev if he would ever try to find out more about his background. As far as he could remember, Bev had replied along the lines that, since his mother had not agreed to see him when he was fourteen years old, it was probably best left alone. I have no recollection of Kate or Philip every asking about his background.

Fragments and constructions

Ian revealed that he had picked up fragments of information over the years from which he had constructed his own account of events. He imagined that Bev's father had been in the American navy and had docked in Southampton at some point, eventually returning to the States. Whether he had thought of him as black he didn't say, but he had gathered that there was money somewhere and that Nan Savage had worked for a well-off family whose daughter had been Bev's mother and that Nan had agreed to take the baby from her. Quite a convincing story! He ended by saying, "But as far as I am concerned, Nan and Grandad Savage have always been my grandparents, and they will always be, whatever you find out."

Chapter 32
SEEING, TOUCHING, HOLDING - NOVEMBER 2000

It was a stormy and changeable morning when we set out from our home in Wiltshire with occasional brilliant sunshine and sudden heavy squally showers. The weather mirrored perfectly our turbulent emotions.

For the first time we drove into the car park of the Nursing Home in Andover and parked up. The rain was beating down on the roof of the car so heavily that we were reluctant to get out. I was not sure if we were waiting for the rain to ease or that our nervousness at meeting Lilian was holding us there. Whatever it was, it kept us sitting there.

We had decided that it would be best for Bev and Lilian to have the first few minutes together without me. Then, if he thought that it was appropriate, I would join them. I urged Bev out of the car and he dashed into the entrance returning a few minutes later to tell me that I would be able to sit in a lounge downstairs while he went up to Lilian's room above.

The meeting
How does one prepare for such a meeting? There is no book of etiquette that guides one through the niceties of meeting your mother when you are sixty

years old and she is almost ninety. We had practised some opening lines and had amused ourselves with trying to do better than commenting on the weather and the state of each other's health.

Whatever will we call her? 'Mrs Fletcher' seemed far too formal and 'Lilian' somewhat too familiar. 'Mother' was out of the question, it had no meaning with this complete stranger and felt inappropriate. And what do you wear for such an occasion, something formal, semi-casual? First impressions count, don't they? So what will impress her? But then we thought she would probably have little choice in what she wears and, anyway, whatever it is, we may not even notice. It's her, this person at the heart of all our searching and longing that we have come to see. It's her face, her eyes, her voice, her gestures, what she says that will stay with us.

I sat downstairs, or rather paced around, making one or two visits to the cloakroom. The only reading material in the lounge was a copy of 'Hello' magazine that a member of staff brought me on a tray with coffee and biscuits telling me, with a mild expression of amusement, that it was essential reading, an experience not to be missed. Well, it's an experience that I've yet to have for there was no way I could concentrate even on the pictures of glittering celebrities paraded there for my entertainment.

What was happening upstairs, that's what I wanted to know! What were they saying to each other?

Later, all Bev could do was to give me a few impressions of those first few moments with his mother. When he rounded the bedroom door and saw her there he was completely lost for words. He walked hesitantly towards her, crouched in front of her and they stared into each other's faces. Were there words? Surely some – but all that he could remember was that after a brief look directly into her old glistening eyes he instinctively reached out to hold her and she responded willingly. Then she repeated several times, "I never thought that this would ever be possible." He held her tenderly because of her frailty. She grasped his jacket with both hands and held on with surprising strength. They stayed like that for who knows how long until they relaxed and again searched each other's expressions, eventually widening their gaze to take in more of the person before them.

After a few moments Bev retreated to a chair opposite hers and they began to talk awkwardly about how remarkable it was that they should eventually meet and Bev thanked her for being willing to see him. "I know how hard it has been for you to agree to see me," he said, "but I hope that you won't regret it." "I've wanted to," she replied, "but I don't want to cause distress to my husband or other members of my family. Although I couldn't contact you, I've never forgotten you."

Her eyes never left him. In fact Bev's lasting impression of his visits to Lilian in the months that followed is that she always seemed to be searching for something in him, always weighing him up, following him around the room with her eyes and, even when I was talking to her, her attention would stray in his direction.

It unnerved him. Was she looking for something or was she just enjoying her son? Bev conjectured that she was trying to establish how much like his father he was and that made him feel under scrutiny; maybe under suspicion. We had thought about the possibility of her feeling a little frightened and suspicious of us, wondering why we had contacted her so late in her life. Did she imagine that we wanted something from her, her money perhaps?

After thirteen and a half minutes Bev came down

I never thought that this would ever be possible. I've never forgotten you.

for me. Quickly I muttered, "How's it going?" "Oh fine, no problem", he reassured me. I'd planned what I might say to start with, something humorous, I thought, about how strange it felt to be trying to impress your mother-in-law when you've already been married for thirty eight years.

We climbed the stairs and walked along a short, brightly carpeted corridor passing closed numbered doors until we reached the corner bedroom at the far end. Bev knocked and opened the door but Lilian remained hidden behind it until we passed into the room and there she was sat out in a chair beside the bed, keen eyed missing nothing. I leaned down to her and we kissed and greeted each other warmly.

She still looked very frail although, from having been only five stone when she came into the home eight months earlier, her health had improved considerably. Her eyes were sparkling and she had a lovely smile.

I kept looking into her face expecting, hoping to see a likeness, some resemblance between her and her long lost son, but I saw nothing to remind me of him. For all my rehearsal of what I would say, I don't recall any of it coming from my lips.

We three were overwhelmed. Time slowed and each movement seemed magnified. We were face to face at last, total strangers with the closest of connections. That might have made us tender and tearful and longing to embrace but instead we looked at each other, searching faces struggling to read what we saw while trying to control our emotions and fumble for appropriate words and gestures that would fill the awkwardness of not knowing where to begin. How does one begin a conversation that could in any way convey what that moment meant and the impact of sixty years apart?

Bev and I had many years of experience of visiting very elderly members of the congregations we served, people whom we had come to love and value. We generally knew them well and they responded to us as their friends. But this could hardly be more different. We were so emotionally invested in Lilian although she was personally unknown to us.

There was no one else present who knew us both and could ease the introduction. We knew more about her than almost any other elderly person we had visited but only now were we beginning to know her, the sound of her voice, the shape of her face, the state of her health, the look in her eyes. I had to keep reminding myself, this is Bev's mother. Waiting for this moment had become a long established habit which was now suddenly at an end – but it didn't feel like that, not yet.

I found a seat near to her and we began to talk about many things while Bev watched and listened attentively. She led the conversation and raised subjects that I would not have raised so soon but they had obviously been on her mind and had troubled her for some time.

She spoke freely of Teddy's faults and after a while I interrupted her and said, "But he was a charming man, wasn't he? Good looking – and you were attracted to him?" "Yes, unfortunately", she replied still appearing to be somewhat wistful as she remembered him. She said more than once that Bev looked like his father and that she had been very worried when we first made contact in case he proved to be too like him. "Teddy was very unreliable, not towards me, but he made things very difficult for my husband who was his boss."

Apparently Ted, despite his assurances, had confessed to her more than once that the baby was not well. She asked Bev if he was able to tell her if he had been a sickly baby and he confirmed what Ted had told her. She told us that she had almost lost him when she was seven months pregnant and she imagined that was why he was so poorly. It became clear to us that she knew almost nothing of what happened to her child after they were separated, or maybe she had forgotten what she once knew. She had not realised that Bev had actually lived with the Foderingham family or that Ted had never admitted to being his father.

In answer to her questions I tried to outline details of Bev's early years but the story soon became too complicated for her to grasp and, anyway, our presence in her room was overwhelming her. It wasn't the time for a detailed account.

I talked to her about her experience as a teacher and she asked whether we had visited her college in Cambridge. When I told her that it was being refurbished, she said, "Yes it needed it." Apparently

she had been asked to stay on at the college at the
end of her training to do some further studies in the
science department but her husband had felt that
it wasn't necessary especially as they were getting
married.

Hector did not come from Scotland, as I had
imagined, but from Lancashire. They had met in
Cambridge at the tennis club. "Oh, you enjoyed
tennis then?" I said. "Oh yes! I love to watch it on
TV," she said adding, "Hector was very good."

Headmistress

She spoke of her time at the Tidworth school and
explained that she had first been the head of the
infants department but, when the Junior Head
suddenly died, she had been asked to take charge of
the entire school, a role that she enjoyed very much.
I told her that I also had trained to be a teacher and,
as one colleague to another, she and I shared our
experiences. She was very surprised to hear that
Teddy had educated his children privately.

I explained to her how Bev had left school with
no qualifications but had studied alone during his
'teens to prepare for college. She asked about his
theological training and the college he attended. She
said that she had been very worried about Bev and
had tried very hard to find a suitable boarding school
for him when he was ten years old.

Bev joined in, "And when you retired you were
doing 'meals on wheels' weren't you?" She laughed,
"However did you know that?" "Well Frank told
us." "Oh yes, and after that I used to weigh the
babies at the clinic."

Family photos

From time to time during the conversation we
glanced around the room and spotted family

This poor man called, and the Lord heard him; he saved him out of all his troubles.

photos hanging on the walls. When we asked about them she was a little vague since she couldn't find her glasses but we gathered that they were of her daughter with her husband and her great grandchildren. Hector was also among them.

I asked her if she had been blonde when she was younger, describing Kate and suggesting that she may have inherited her looks and colouring. "No, I don't think so. I wasn't particularly fair," she said. So my theory proved incorrect but I do have one more. Maybe Bev's Grandmother, Kate, is the little blonde I am looking for.

As our visit came to an end Bev asked if he could read a few verses from the Bible and Lilian agreed. He had chosen to read part of Psalm 34 which contains the words, "Glorify the Lord with me: Let us exalt his name together … This poor man called, and the Lord heard him; he saved him out of all his troubles." Then he prayed and as he did so he mentioned the possibility of an ongoing relationship between us. At the end Lilian looked very thoughtful and then said, "So you will be coming again?" To which Bev replied, "Only if you want us to." "Oh yes," she said. "I would like that very much." We suggested we return in two weeks' time and she said, "I shall look forward to it." At that point a member of staff came into the room offering to bring Lilian's lunch to her. Bev said, "We're not staying any longer. We don't want to tire you out." To which Lilian replied, "Oh, that won't do me any harm."

Meeting Mrs Heron

As we made our way back down the stairs Mrs Heron was hovering at the bottom. She was obviously very keen to meet us and was curious about how our meeting had gone. She had never been in a situation like this and was interested to find out how it was that we had found Lilian.

We sat in the privacy of her office trying to relate the story of our search as briefly as we could. She was fascinated by it and asked many questions. Eventually she began to volunteer information about Lilian and her daughter. Lilian had been very poorly when she first came into their care and had been unable to swallow. She had been nursed in her room since she was not expected to live. However, she had made a remarkable recovery although she remains weak and is nursed on a ripple bed as she is so thin. She goes to bed around 6 pm but always reads her newspaper. Sometimes someone from the Baptist Church comes to see her. Her daughter, who is fair and freckly, is very chatty and has an outgoing personality.

An hour later we left to continue our journey to stay with friends in Bournemouth, sixty miles away.

We drove the Hampshire roads hardly noticing passing sights, our minds preoccupied with the events of the morning. We shared an unspoken relief and sense of gratitude that the first visit was over and that it had gone so well.

After a while Bev confessed that he felt a slight sense of anti-climax. Seeing Lilian had become so important to him that his expectations were, perhaps, always going to fall short of the reality. We had found her only just in time. Her memory is fading and she is frail and tired. It is almost certainly too late to get to know her well or to share with her many details of our life. But we had met her and she had responded as a mother would to a son with whom she was once pregnant and to whom she gave life – and that was very special indeed.

Chapter 33
SNAPSHOTS EN ROUTE
- NOVEMBER 2000

23rd November 2000 - No problem!

From Bournemouth, Bev 'phoned Ian. The call was partly to update him on our visit to Lilian but mainly to check how he and Suzie had been coping with all that we had told them on our recent visit.

It was an exciting conversation. Not only had they discussed the story at length after we had left but they had also talked quite freely to their friends about it. Ian described Suzie as being 'full of it' and spoke of how she had already told her mother and step-father.

Unknown to us, even before we went to see them, Ian had told his golfing friends that his parents were coming to tell him 'where he came from' – so typical of his sense of humour! After our visit he had kept them guessing about his ancestry for some time which led them to some creative speculation. This in turn led to some of his friends revealing secrets of their own, one divulging that her mother was Indian.

In a strange way it came as something of a comfort to know that even young people find it hard to face up to their mixed race identity. We were relieved to hear Ian so matter-of-fact about his history. He

You mean you've never even seen her before?

had clearly enjoyed the experience of revealing it to his friends but we may never know what he really thought and felt deep down.

Bev seized the opportunity to ask him how much of a problem his colouring had been for him growing up, a subject that we had never raised between us. It seemed easier to ask him at the end of a 'phone than face to face.

He said that it had been difficult at times, especially at school but he pointed out that other youngsters had been teased, even abused by racists. He was keen to reassure us that since he had left school it had never been a problem at all. In fact it had been a bonus to have a tan when his friends were trying hard to get one! He was characteristically funny and relaxed about it all and we felt a burden lift as, at last, we could discuss the subject openly.

Talking of our visit to Lilian, he expressed amazement, "You mean you've never even seen her before?" He still seemed confused about Bev's childhood, but then who could blame him?

24th November 2000 – Sharing Mum!
Today we took the ferry from Southampton to the Isle of Wight to visit Phyllis' sister, Lily, and Bob, her husband. We travelled with Sheila and Syd and we all understood that the purpose of the visit was, in part at least, to share with them what we had discovered.

Sitting on the ferry Bev took the opportunity to talk with Sheila about their relationship with Phyllis. She had always felt closer to Aunt Lily than to her own Mum and, when Phyllis had died the previous year, she could see that this had affected Bev more deeply than her. She felt this had unsettled him and so she was not surprised that he now had this need to find his birth mother.

Phyllis had been so determined to fight for Bev's protection as a child that Sheila had less of her than she might have expected. She had never expressed this to us before and was immediately keen to reassure us that she had never been jealous of him because she knew that he needed the security that Phyllis could give him. She already enjoyed that security. We realised in that moment what a strain it must have been on her as her young 'brother' had come and gone over the years and we remembered something that she had said to Bev when Phyllis was dying. "We should never have been separated you and me, should we?"

Bev was obviously very moved by this revelation and told her of his love for her for freely sharing her Mum with him and for being there for him. It was a touching moment, and another healing by-product from our search.

6th December 2000 – Photos galore!
We were a little late but Lilian was waiting for us and seemed pleased to see us today. She was relaxed and seemed more at ease when I was present. I had taken photographs of Bev's early life which I thought would please her and help to prompt her memory.

She immediately recognised the earliest photo we have of him in the arms of a nurse taken in the grounds of the Woodlands Nursing Home and recalled being driven there, heavily pregnant, during an air raid. The nurse in the photo was the one who erected a screen to prevent flying debris and shattered glass landing on the mothers and their babies if bombs fell.

She said that Teddy and her husband had difficulty driving to see her because of the bombing on Southampton and once they had ended up in a ditch. Bev's birth was straightforward but her fall before he was born had frightened her. She thought that he was about 8 lbs. at birth. She had no recollection of how long Bev was in the nursing home after his birth but did recall visiting him with Michael.

I risked asking, "Did you and Hector ever consider keeping Bev with you as your son?" She replied very simply, "It was never discussed." I found this rather hard to hear because it made her seem too ready to give him up and to accept empty reassurances from a man whom she knew to be unreliable.

We went on to look at photos that were taken when Bev was at Tiptree and Woodford and I told her about the White family and Mill Grove. She seemed enthralled by the story and especially to hear of the way in which the Home had never appealed for money but had always been fully supported by the voluntary giving of Christian people.

// What are you?

We pored over other photographs until it became obvious that Lilian was growing tired and it was time for us to leave. Bev again offered to read and pray with her before we left, at which she suddenly said, "What are you?" The directness of the question took him by surprise. He tried to explain that he was a Christian minister who was no longer working in one church but with many, but whether his answer satisfied her is doubtful.

Her fixed gaze and this sudden question seemed to confirm what he had felt from the beginning, that he was under suspicion. Did she suspect that he was like her former lover, his father, manipulative, dishonest and looking for something from her.

Bev took a couple of photos of her and we were about to kiss her goodbye when she began to talk about the other residents in the home. There were some twenty of them and, although Lilian had her meals with them, she didn't often go into the lounge for, as she explained, "They are all old people, who are mostly sleeping and snoring." We all saw the funny side of this and laughed with her. She had only just reminded us of her great age.

10th December 2000 – The Headmistress

Maureen from Tidworth Post Office telephoned today with good news. She had talked to a woman who had taught at the Garrison School under Lilian's headship in the nineteen sixties and was able to give me her telephone number.

I 'phoned her and found Ann a mine of information. She had taught in the Junior part of the Garrison School under a former headmistress, Mrs Elms, while Lilian was Head of the Infants. Mrs Elms had been a strong and demanding Head Teacher and so everyone was shocked when she died very suddenly. It was then that Lilian was appointed Head Teacher of both Junior and Infants departments. At that time the school had over 300 children in it with several classes of 48 children. Ann said that, although Lilian continued to maintain high standards, she instituted a much friendlier regime. She found her very approachable, a person in whom she could confide and, although they were not exactly close friends, they did have an enjoyable working relationship. When Ann left to work with families of the British Army in Cyprus in 1967, Lilian went out twice to visit her, each time without Hector.

20th December 2000 – Christmas visit

Since we were travelling to exchange Christmas gifts with our families in Bishopstoke, we took a slight detour to visit Lilian today. Before we set out we chatted about what Bev should take as his first gift to his mother. A large bouquet of flowers perhaps? Chocolates? Something impressive to show his pleasure in finding her? No! That couldn't be. Her daughter would visit later in the day and, if she found an unexpectedly large gift in Lilian's room, she would certainly ask where it had come from and who was responsible. In the event we gave her a book on the Psalms by Dr John Stott and just a little chocolate which could soon disappear.

Lilian was waiting for us when we entered her room and she looked much better than when we had last seen her. She told us that she had put on 2 stone in weight since she entered the nursing home in March and was now over 7 stone. Her hair had been permed and she was wearing an attractive green outfit and seemed relaxed and happy.

She had enjoyed carol singing in the lounge and had laughed with the staff at the rather hit-and-miss accompaniment of a lady on a small keyboard.

She added that she was surprised that some of the residents had forgotten the carol singing by the next day. We couldn't help but smile and be thankful that her mind was still so sharp.

The carol singing had been quite an outing for her since she hadn't left her room much or been involved at all in any social event in the home since she entered it ten months earlier. And soon she would have another outing when a taxi would arrive at 9 o'clock on Christmas day to take her home to her husband and family for a little while. She would return to have Christmas lunch in the nursing home.

We spoke of her memories of Christmas and of her sister, Grace, who was four years older than she. "She was a terror when she was a child", she said. "She eventually married a man of forty who had an uncertain temper. Their third child was handicapped, his hands were burnt. Mother thought it had happened in the hospital but I don't know. It didn't seem likely."

Grace remained in Cambridge into her adult life and worked as an administrator in Peterhouse College. She had two daughters but Lilian had lost contact with them.

Bev enquired more about Michael. She said he was very good looking and had worked at one time on the ferries travelling between Southampton and the French ports. He suddenly died of a heart attack it seems, but the precise details had either faded from her memory or she preferred not to share them. She was home alone when news of his death came through.

She was pleased to hear about Ann, the teacher who was once a member of staff under her Headship. She came alive as she described the two trips that she made to visit Ann in Cyprus. She had travelled abroad many times, always on her own because Hector wasn't keen on travelling, his disability no doubt making it difficult for him to be away from home.

Bev gently broached the subject of whether her daughter might like to know of him. Might she be upset if she didn't have a chance to hear about her brother from her mother's own lips? Lilian was thoughtful for a moment then said, "She knows nothing about Teddy and me, that we were close. She wouldn't believe it of me." Bev said, "You and your daughter are very close aren't you?" "Oh. Yes", she said. "It's lovely to have a daughter, isn't it?" We heartily agreed.

The deception of our secret visits was beginning to feel uncomfortable and we speculated about how long it would be before we were discovered and what the Fletcher family's attitude would be towards us. However, there was nothing that we could do about the situation without Lilian's agreement, and her mind seemed to be made up – she would not reveal our presence to her family.

However, a brief conversation as we left the home that day led Mrs Heron to confide that she thought that Lilian's attitude was changing and that she might come round to telling her daughter. If that were to happen we stood to gain much more insight into the family history and into Lilian's life, but it was fraught with danger.

Chapter 34

INSIDER INFORMATION
- MARCH 2001

I stumbled across the name Megan Foderingham
one day in a telephone directory and rang to
enquire if she had any connection with Ted and
Marjorie. I was getting used to approaching complete
strangers by now and being less anxious meant that
I could put them at their ease and get them to accept
me more easily.

I was fascinated to discover that Megan had been
married to Steven, Ted and Marjorie's son, but they
divorced some twenty years earlier. She was very
surprised by my call and understandably reluctant
to give me any information, advising me to approach
the family directly.

However, she listened long enough for me
to explain who I was and why I had phoned.
Eventually she said, "I was married into the family
for several years, but I don't ever recall anyone
mentioning the name Beverley, not even my
husband."

But as the conversation continued and she began to
think back, she changed her mind. "Actually, I have
heard that name. Now where did I hear it? I think
it was probably my mother who spoke of a child by
that name. My Grandparents lived in Bournemouth

Road, Chandlers Ford, and my parents lived with them in the war years. They knew Edwin and Daisy Froud in Leigh Road, so I guess that they must have known of Beverley. Yes! I vaguely remember them saying something about the Frouds being too old to have such a young boy living with them." So, little by little, Megan began to share the memories that came swimming back to her.

She recalled how Marjorie had given the impression to her parents that she and Ted owned the bungalow and that Daisy had been her children's nanny, but her family knew that couldn't be true since the Frouds had lived there long before Ted and Marjorie had come on the scene. It had always puzzled them why they continued to live in the bungalow when Marjorie was unable to say a kind word about the Frouds.

The Foderingham daughter-in law

Megan confided that she was never considered an acceptable daughter-in-law by Ted and Marjorie because, although she was bright and well educated, she was raised on a Council estate.

She had fond memories of Ted but had found it very difficult to relate to Marjorie who was critical of her and condescending. "It was true," she said, "Marjorie was a wronged woman in many ways. She knew very little about Ted when they married. He introduced himself to her family as the Honourable Edward Foderingham, and told them that he had no living relatives, but then relatives began to pop up all over the place."

Apparently, Ted's sister and her West Indian husband suddenly appeared on their doorstep in Bishopstoke one day and the black connection was there for all to see. Only recently Megan's daughter went abroad on holiday with her father, Steven, and someone introduced themselves to them as their relations. They had spotted the unusual surname in the hotel register. "So you see," she concluded, "whatever Marjorie wants us all to believe, the truth will out."

I told her about Marjorie's denial of any West Indian Grandfather, to which Megan replied, "Oh, yes! Well mother-in-law could easily swear that black was white - excuse the pun."

Younger members of the family had openly discussed the likelihood of a black ancestor somewhere in their past and had no problem with the idea, but Marjorie's prejudices just couldn't tolerate the notion. When Megan gave birth to her daughter, she and Steven hatched a plan to pretend that the black baby in the next room was theirs! It was as well for Marjorie they didn't carry out their plan. She may not have survived the trauma.

Megan was not altogether surprised to hear of Bev's existence but she was genuinely shocked that his childhood had been so sad and found it hard to believe that Ted would stand by and do nothing when he was put into a children's home. She instinctively blamed Marjorie for what happened until I reminded her that it seemed unlikely that she had known anything of Bev's existence until after she arrived in Chandlers Ford.

She asked me what we intended to do with all the information we had collected. It was a good question. What will we do with it? I could only respond by saying that it was a decision for Bev to make. She asked whether I thought she should tell her daughter about our conversation. I advised against it on the grounds that she might then feel inclined to tackle her father about it and cause upset in the family. I told her that I had asked Marjorie for some photographs of Ted and she had refused. She

> Whatever Marjorie wants us all to believe, the truth will out.

**I don't
doubt your
story for a
moment.**

seemed touched by this and said, "Of course Bev
must have some photos. I will send you some of our
wedding. They are rather dated but at least they give
you some idea of how we all once looked."

After I had replaced the receiver, I wondered how
Megan would feel about our conversation after she
had time to reflect on it. I imagined that she would
find it very hard not to share what I had told her, and
she might change her mind about sending photos.

If fact, several weeks passed and, having not heard
from Megan, I was beginning to wonder whether my
conjectures were coming true when one day in early
April the 'phone rang and it was Megan.

"I am so sorry for the delay", she said. "I managed
to find my wedding album in the loft but have not
been able to remove the photos from it because
they have been stuck there for such a long time. I'm
thinking of sending it to you as it is. Would that be
OK with you?"

"Thanks so much, Megan", I replied. "We really
don't want to put you to more trouble. We would
be willing to collect it from your home or, maybe
we could meet up somewhere?" She readily agreed
to this suggestion and we arranged to be in contact
again to arrange a time after I had looked at Bev's
diary.

"Megan, I feel the need to reassure you that we
have no ulterior motive in asking this of you," I
said, and was about to say more along that line
when she interrupted. "I don't doubt your story for
a moment," she said. "Since we last talked I have
spoken to my mother and, although she is now in
her 80s, she has a clear memory of Beverley and the
Frouds and the stories that Marjorie told them."

It was Wednesday April 25th before we talked
again. Bev and I planned to visit Lilian two days
later and hoped that Megan would be free to meet

us after the visit. It was a brief call. Megan needed
to make some changes to her schedule before she
could commit to a meeting and would get back to us
but then, just before she hung up, she asked again
whether we would mind if she told her daughter
about our contact.

We had already speculated that this might happen
and so I was able to agree on the understanding
that they wouldn't speak to other members of the
Foderingham family about it. I explained that my
contact with Marjorie had made Bev quite reluctant
to have further contact with them.

Megan rang back the next evening and we
arranged to meet at 2pm the next day at the Lily
Langtry Tea Rooms in Stockbridge. She then
surprised me by saying that she had told her
daughter, Katharine, about us. She had come to stay
with her mother for a few days and would we mind
if she came to meet us as well. I readily agreed to the
suggestion but when I told Bev he looked somewhat
alarmed. "Whatever will we talk about?" he said.

Chapter 35

LILY LANGTRY TEA ROOMS
- APRIL 2001

After visiting Lilian we drove the 15 miles
south to Stockbridge to meet Megan and
Katharine. It was a pleasant sunny afternoon
and there was a feeling of spring in the air as we
drove through the delightful Test valley where
swollen rivers reminded us of recent floods.

We arrived slightly early so we drove slowly along
the length of the long straight High Street searching
for the tea rooms. We were both feeling slightly
nervous, not quite knowing what to expect from
these strangers.

We parked up and peered into the tea rooms but
could see no one who looked as though they might
be waiting for us. We had only a vague description
to go by. "We're both quite tall, Katharine has short,
curly fair hair and mine is sort of brown. We'll be
driving a Vauxhall Corsa."

While we waited Bev wandered off absent-
mindedly window shopping to pass the time. But
it was not long before a car fitting the description
came to a halt outside the tea rooms. Katharine
stepped out, a tall, slender and attractive figure
in the sunshine. Megan followed, a striking well-
dressed woman looking rather less relaxed than her

daughter.

Bev returned to where I was standing and together we approached them and shook hands rather formally. Megan began to apologise for being a little late but Katharine broke in and said to Bev, "You look so like my father. As soon as we saw you from the car we knew, didn't we Mum? We both said 'that's him'."

Katherine takes charge

Katharine was a gift to us that afternoon. Her evident enjoyment of the occasion and her youthful confidence engulfed the nervous people around her and she quickly took the lead to a small courtyard at the rear of the property and to a table next to a stream.

We chose our drinks and Bev went off to collect them while Katharine talked easily, relaxing us with her warm and friendly chatter. When Megan reached for the bag in which she had brought the wedding album, she gently touched her mother's arm indicating that she should leave it be so that we could just talk for a while. And talk we did - for two and half hours.

I began by asking Katharine about herself, where she lived and what she is doing. She laughed and said, "The answer to that question is rather long and complicated." It transpired that, having gained a degree in anthropology from Manchester University, at twenty five years of age, she headed off on an eighteen month tour of the world.

She had only recently returned and was currently living between York and Megan's home in Southampton. She would begin a new job soon, working for a charity. I gathered that, such was her interest in meeting a long lost uncle, she had travelled the two hundred and fifty miles from York especially for the occasion.

Soon our conversation turned to her family, especially to her grandparents. She amused us all when she described Marjorie as being a cross between Rose Nylund, the dumb fluffy blonde in the American comedy series, 'The Golden Girls', and Hyacinth Bucket, a surname which she insists is to be pronounced 'Bouquet', in the British comedy series, 'Keeping up Appearances'.

Megan seemed happy to let her daughter manage the conversation but came into her own when the wedding album was eventually produced. "Spot Grandmother!" said Katharine. "She's the one with the bird's nest on her head."

There we saw the Foderingham family laid out before us as they appeared thirty years ago, Ted and Marjorie, Steven and Megan and one bridesmaid, the Foderingham's eldest daughter, Patricia, who was blonde, attractive and already married.

I was surprised that Ted had changed so much from my memories of him. He appeared much older than his sixty four years, his age when the photos were taken. I had always imagined that Bev was like him looking younger than his years but Ted's chronic diabetes had clearly affected him. He had put on weight and his hair was grey and thinning, combed back and anchored against his skull whereas I recall him being thin and with dark curly hair. He stood taller than his son who looked rather darker skinned than Bev but with very light, perhaps grey eyes which Katharine had inherited.

I asked, "Wasn't there another daughter?" "Oh yes," said Megan. "Sadly Vivian went away to study at Reading University and while there she became pregnant. Marjorie found that hard to cope with and was very unkind to her. I seem to remember that she found reasons not to attend the wedding which was very sad to us."

Photographs of guests revealed that Doris, Ted's sister, and her husband, Wilf, had attended and he was noticeably dark skinned. I looked for representatives from Marjorie's Welsh family, but there was not a clerical collar to be seen. Megan said that they had simply disappeared from the family.

Many more intriguing revelations filled that sunny afternoon including facts about the grandchildren and Marjorie's social life as a widow. Surprisingly, she had become a member of a yacht club but her interest had little to do with boats.

When I showed them a photograph of Bev as a child in the garden of the bungalow in Chandlers Ford with Patricia, his younger half- sibling, they exclaimed, "We would recognise her anywhere. She still looks very similar to that."

The conversation turned inevitably to Steven. Katharine was born in 1974 when he was twenty nine. "He was not a philanderer but he was immature," Megan said. "We called him 'Peter Pan'". I was struck by that because I had sometimes called Bev by that name, not because of his immaturity, but because he continues to look young for his years.

Steven left when Katherine was twenty months old and they were divorced ten months later. Marjorie's advice at the time still echoed in Megan's memory, "Well, when there's no love left in a marriage, it is best for it to end." Megan had protested at the time that she thought that she had married for life – and there was now a child to be considered, but it made no difference. Foderingham men were not good at honouring their promises.

Steven went on to marry again three years later but Megan never did commit herself again. Despite her best efforts to keep in touch, Katherine saw too little of her father while she was growing up although she clearly continues to love him and visits him from time to time.

I am interested in spiritual things, you know.

It was obviously sad for Megan to pour over photographs of her wedding day again and we couldn't help but notice how strained she looked.

Bev said very little throughout the afternoon but did eventually remark that he was not at all sure that a meeting with his half-brother would ever be possible or useful. "I don't wish to crash into people's lives after so many years have passed and they are settled," he said. At this Katharine came alive and, looking directly at him she said, "I want you to know that it is very important for me to meet you. You are part of my family. You're my uncle." It was moving to hear this member of the Foderingham family acknowledge him.

Then she went on to take us all by surprise by saying, "I'm probably going to get a knock over the head for this but knowing my father as I do, how reserved he is, the nuances of his character and how he thinks, I saw him at his restaurant yesterday and told him about you. He was not at all sure whether to believe me. All he said was, "How do you know it's true?" I couldn't answer him, of course, not then.

"He's ill, you know, and could die. He will need some time to sit with this. We will have to be patient. I wanted to see him before he went away on holiday today to give him time to think about it all. He was very fond of his father." And then she added, "I am interested in spiritual things, you know."

This last sentence immediately aroused our curiosity and we gently probed to see what her interest was. It took less than a minute to discover that both Megan and Katherine had contact with Christians whom we knew and that they had attended churches with which we were also familiar. Bev had been in contact only two weeks previously with a minister who lived just across the road from Megan.

This was Bev's opportunity to explain how his time at Mill Grove had affected him. "I don't feel resentful or bitter about what happened to me", he said. "While I was in the Children's Home people taught me about Christ and what he had done for me and I came to trust him. He changed my outlook and has been at the centre of my life ever since that time."

We then went on to tell them of our search so far and of how we came to find Lilian, describing her and telling of her love for Ted. They listened intently.

Eventually it was time to leave. We stood outside and watched them drive slowly away from the Lily Langtry Tea Rooms wondering if we would ever see them again.

As we settled into our car it suddenly struck us how ironic it was that we had met in a place named after a lady who became famous for her dalliance with King Edward VII. Nearly a hundred years after their affair we had spent an afternoon rehearsing a similar story of another Lily and Edward, Bev's mother and father.

Chapter 36

DISCOVERED
- SEPTEMBER 2002

O ur monthly visits to Lilian became part of the routine of our lives over the next two years, some yielded snippets of new information but there was less and less carry-over from one conversation to another and we found ourselves rehearsing the same details and answering similar questions each time.

Lilian had made a supreme effort to receive us and to answer my many questions. Our contact had awakened her and had given her reason to rally her thoughts and talk about things of which she had never spoken for many decades. She seemed to have been rejuvenated by the experience and we were glad for that. But she was getting tired and her energy for conversation was declining although she never would have admitted it.

The visitors' book

It was on a visit in late September 2002 that we learned that the Herons were to sell the nursing home and move away. Since Mrs Heron was nowhere to be found when we arrived, we signed the visitors' book as visitors for Mrs Fletcher. We scarcely remembered doing it. If we had we might simply

Son! What son? have regarded it as a small change of detail that was harmless enough. But it proved to be far more significant than we could have imagined.

When June signed in as usual later that day she noticed the names of the two visitors who had visited her mother and, although she was in a hurry, she commented on it to Lilian asking who her visitors had been.

Lilian was taken by surprise. What exactly she said in reply we will never know in detail but apparently she simply blurted out the fact that her son had found her and had been visiting and June should meet him. Her son! What son? June knew nothing of a son except her older brother who had died. Mother must be delirious. Anyway, she had no time to talk about it then and left soon after concerned for her mother's state of mind.

Meanwhile, we were in Llandudno, North Wales, on holiday. The first we knew that something was amiss was when Mrs. Heron left a message on Bev's mobile phone asking him to call her as soon as possible. We conjectured that Lilian may have suddenly become ill, or maybe she had died, so we called her back as soon as we discovered her message.

We sat high up on the Great Orme, a prominent limestone headland above Llandudno, looking out over the sea as Mrs Heron broke the news that June had spoken of her concerns for her mother and in consequence the two of them had spent two hours together during which time Mrs Heron had revealed all.

Revelations and their consequences

June was understandably nonplussed and very upset. She knew nothing of another child in the family and found it very hard to believe that her mother would have kept such a secret from her. If her father came to know of the secret visits he would be too frail to handle it.

In making her sudden revelations Lilian seemed not to have anticipated that June would be distressed. She became angry because June was not immediately happy for her and wasn't at all sure that she would want to meet a half-brother, even if the story proved to be true, which she doubted very much.

When we arrived home from our holiday a short letter from Lilian was waiting for us. It explained briefly what had happened but it portrayed a very different picture to that which Mrs Heron had conveyed. According to Lilian she had simply told June everything and, although shocked, she had taken it very well.

Bev was due to go to America the following Tuesday, October 8th, but before he went he wrote to Lilian assuming that she would show his letter to June.

No doubt June and her mother continued to discuss the situation and June would have many questions about us, so in his letter Bev made it clear that she should feel no pressure to make contact with us.

We understood what a shock she had suffered and that she would need time to come to terms with the situation. He also explained that we didn't want anything from Lilian or from any members of the family. Our search had one purpose only, to enable him to have some sense of his roots. The letter posted, Bev was then away from home for two weeks.

Around the time of his return we received a further letter from Lilian which she had absent-mindedly sent to Lenore, the Canadian lady who used to visit their home, who guessed it was for us and sent it on. Lilian said she was very depressed and worried about Bev in case he was ill from all his travels and, she assumed, that was why it had been so long since we had visited her. I wrote back assuring her that Bev was in good health and that we'd visit her as soon as possible.

Lilian in distress and her family alarmed

It was October 31st when we took the now familiar journey to the home. She appeared more confused than usual and her speech seemed slurred. She confirmed Mrs Heron's account of what happened. June had been upset and Lilian had herself cried all one evening.

It had been over a month since her outburst but they had not once talked about the subject since then. This was an altogether more worrying visit. We had hoped to find that Lilian and June had talked at length and that June had come to understand why there had been such secrecy and was more prepared to deal with the situation. But instead we were alarmed at how she might be feeling and how she might react to us if there was contact.

After we arrived home from our visit I called Mrs Heron. She told us that, as might be expected, June had told her husband, and her son and daughter about what had happened and the family had discussed the situation.

June was still finding it very hard to accept that she had been denied knowledge of her sibling all her life. She was so disturbed that she had consulted a solicitor about how to handle the situation if Bev began to make demands of the family, so she clearly feared the worse. Like her mother, she was also concerned not to deceive her father but Mrs Heron had the impression that she did intend to make contact with us eventually. She even suggested that her daughter, Kelly, might accompany her to meet us.

Mrs Heron confirmed that the Nursing Home would be handed over to new owners within the month and hearing this also troubled me since, with her departure, we would lose our one mediator with June. I sent a card with our names, address and telephone number on it requesting Mrs Heron to place it in Lilian's file so that we could be informed should anything happen to either Lilian or Hector.

It was far from clear to us what might happen next. We felt that we had no choice but to continue our visits to Lilian. We couldn't abandon her now whatever the family might think of us.

We signed the visitors' book leaving evidence of our visits for June to see and hoped that she would be prompted to make contact with us but several weeks went by without a word from her. Had we alienated June from her mother? If so, perhaps we had a responsibility to attempt to heal the breach. Or would it be best to let matters rest where they were?

I couldn't let the matter rest so on November 15th I wrote to June. I had no certainty that Lilian had shown her the letter that Bev had sent to her so I thought that at least I should confirm what he had written. I also hoped that she would be able to be more accepting of him if she knew more about what had happened to him in his childhood and why we had set out on this quest.

A few days after receiving my letter, June replied. She said that she was in a state of shock and needed time to come to terms with what Lilian had told her. It was, of course, an entirely understandable reaction and we couldn't help but feel for her. A few weeks later, however, she wrote to Bev and from then on they began to correspond by e-mail.

It was far from clear to us what might happen next.

SOMEBODY'S SON

Chapter 37

MARLBOROUGH - JANUARY 2003

June was ready to meet Bev early in the New Year and asked to see him alone. They met in Marlborough, a beautiful town midway between our homes. It was a bitterly cold, overcast day when they sat facing each other across the table in a small café in the town's wide High Street with its arcades, coaching inns and a church at each end.

Bev later described her as fairly tall with greying hair, a straightforward person without airs and graces. She had no accent to speak of and was articulate and confident although quite suspicious of him.

It had been three months since she had learned the secret of his existence during which time she had struggled to adjust to the news which was clearly impacting her perceptions of her mother, her childhood and life in the Fletcher household.

Her long held view of herself as the disadvantaged child of the family was given even more credence by this sudden turn of events. Aunts and uncles loved her brother, Michael, but not her. And now it turns out that even her parents had her as a substitute for the baby that they had given up. When she saw Bev's birth certificate with Hector's name on it, she said,

❞❞This is really bizarre

"They should have kept you."

She said repeatedly, "This is really bizarre." The family secret had, it seems, already become something of an obsession with her. She was most shocked by the fact that her father had always put Lilian on a pedestal and had spoken disparagingly of a woman known to the family who had been unfaithful to her husband. It now seemed unbelievable to her that he could do that given their own experience. Was all her history a lie?

Hector adored Lilian and would do anything to keep her happy. Perhaps the latest revelation explained why. Was he afraid of losing her again?

June felt that her parents had blotted out the entire event from their minds; it was as though it had never happened. However, Bev gently pointed out to her that the fact of his existence came up more than once in their marriage. Lilian had been approached for help when Daisy Froud was dying and she had met Phyllis in the solicitor's office in Andover when Bev was nearly fifteen years of age. Several times June expressed her distress at being shut out of these important events in the life of her family. It was a distressing conversation for them both.

Suspicions

June's husband and son were very suspicious of the appearance of this so-called half-brother and immediately questioned what he might be after and why he had turned up at this late stage in their lives. But her husband had also greeted the news of his mother-in-law's indiscretion with some humour.

Apparently, he came from a rather dysfunctional family himself and had always thought of the Fletchers as appearing superior, respectable and highly moral, so he was amused to hear of the skeleton in their cupboard. Above all father and son were set on sending a clear warning to the intrusive stranger that he had better not do anything to upset Grandad or he would have them to deal with.

They could see no reason why June should meet Bev. Their sympathy was reserved alone for Hector and they levelled the total blame for what had happened at Ted Foderingham whom they judge guilty of deliberately trying to destroy their parents' and grandparents' marriage.

Lilian's care

As they warmed themselves over coffee in the café, June began to relax as she related a story of how Lilian came to be in the nursing home. When she fell and broke her hip she was only four stone in weight. The operation that followed was not very successful and she faced a second procedure when she was stronger.

Then without warning June received a telephone call informing her that the hospital was to discharge Lilian because it could do nothing more for her. She was not expected to live more than two or three weeks so, after a frantic search, June found a temporary nursing home for her.

The family agreed that, in the event of her death, no attempt should be made to resuscitate her. But despite all the odds against it, she pulled through. "She is over seven stone in weight now and much better in herself" she said. "I believe that has happened because you came into her life. You've done that!"

Bev pointed out the amazing timing of so many aspects of the story of our search and spoke of God's direction in it all, to which June responded, "Oh, yes. It was meant to be. You only found my parents' names in the Electoral Role because for some reason my father completed the form not me.

> She is over seven stone in weight and much better in herself. I believe that has happened because you came into her life. You've done that!

Had I completed it, as I normally did, I would have requested that their names were not publicised and you may never have met mother."

Bev and June were together almost four hours during which time she handed him a photograph album for him to take away and study at his leisure. The meeting was emotionally demanding for them both but no immediate sibling bond materialised to suggest that their relationship would develop into something much closer. A peck on the cheek brought it to an end. In the following months we met members of June's family and, given time and opportunity, deeper relationships may have grown between us but it was not be.

Two photos reunited

Three weeks later we were with Lilian again and she was obviously delighted and relieved that her two children had met at last. Apparently, June had told her mother that she liked Bev, much to her surprise. We showed Lilian the photograph album and it provided another stimulus to her memory and more stories emerged.

We were particularly keen to show her two photos from different sources that we placed side by side. One was of Bev in the arms of a nurse outside the nursing home in the New Forest and the other of Michael who appeared to be in the same garden. On the reverse was marked 'March 1941'. Were those two photographs taken on the same day? "Oh yes", she said. "I remember that day very well. I took Michael to see the baby." Lilian would have been pregnant at the time so June was there too that day!

Chapter 38

MARLBOROUGH AGAIN
- MARCH 2003

Irregular email communication continued between
June and Bev and pressure built for a second
meeting between them.

Bev indicated that he would like me to be included
but June was clearly reluctant to agree. In the end it
was decided that they would meet alone for the first
hour or so then I would join them for lunch so we
returned to Marlborough as before.

June had many questions after her first meeting
with Bev. I imagined she would be curious about
what had happened to him as a child and how his
life had worked out. In fact, she mainly wanted to
talk about the sermon that he had preached at the
Mill Grove Centenary service in Tiptree.

Fallout from the sermon
Lilian had given her the copy of the Home's annual
publication, 'Links', in which an outline of Bev's
sermon had been published. June and other family
members had read it and come to the conclusion that
the preacher seemed very bitter, seeing himself as a
victim and having many problems to resolve.

June explained that this had made her feel as
though he was blaming her family for what had

'... but God intended it for good'. happened to him. That had made her very nervous about meeting him the first time since she suspected that he was looking for revenge.

It appeared that the family had focused on Bev's comments on Joseph's words, 'You intended to harm me' rather than on the main point of the sermon, '... but God intended it for good'. Bev was at pains to explain this to June but whether she accepted or understood what he was saying we were not at all sure. By the time I joined them June was quite tearful while Bev explained that he had never felt any bitterness about his childhood and was certainly not looking for anything more than information and a conciliatory meeting with long lost relatives.

Admittedly he regretted his lack of education and when he learned of Grandfather Briggs' and of Lilian's lifetime in teaching, he imagined that he might have learned so much from them. June showed little sympathy for such thoughts saying that she doubted if their mother or grandfather would have helped him. They hardly ever saw the family in Cambridge and, in her experience, the only educational encouragement she had received from her mother was to follow her into teaching.

Twins
One completely new piece of information that came to light was that when June was two years old Lilian had given birth to twin girls. They were born prematurely and lived long enough to be given names, but June could not remember them and neither Lilian nor Hector had ever spoken of them. They were buried somewhere in Chandlers Ford and June had once talked of going to visit their graves but she never did.

After another four hour marathon, we left. It would be many months before we met again.

❝❝ It's hard for me to realise that you are the baby that I left behind all those years ago.

Chapter 39

ONE DOOR CLOSES... - AUGUST 2004

It was in the summer of 2004 when we made one of our periodic visits to Lilian this time to wish her a happy 93rd birthday. She was in good spirits and looked well and Bev took a photo of her with his new digital camera given him by the family for his birthday ten days earlier. He showed her the photo of herself and others stored in the camera including one of our youngest grandson's thanksgiving and some of our recent trip to Chicago.

This was not the day to tell her, but our lives were about to change significantly. By an amazing series of events we found ourselves receiving, and accepting an invitation to move to Arlington Heights in the North West suburbs of Chicago, Illinois, USA. The move would take us some 4000 miles away from Andover and soon we would say our final goodbyes to Lilian, but not today. That would need to be handled sensitively at another time. Today was her day to celebrate another milestone in her long journey.

Following him with her eyes as she always did, she suddenly said, "It's hard for me to realise that you are the baby that I left behind all those years ago." This was the first time that she had said such a thing and we found it strangely comforting to hear it from her own lips. We wondered if she had made that connection at all since her lapses of memory and the re-running of conversations seemed to suggest that she had only a vague grasp of the relationship between the past and the present, but there was no doubting today that she knew exactly who Bev was.

We had two purposes to our journey that day, to spend time with Lilian, and then to meet June and maybe other members of her family. After an hour we left the nursing home and drove a short distance to the car park of a thatched pub with its beautiful summer flowers and a spacious garden.

Meeting the family

June had suggested nearly eighteen months previously that it would be good for us to have lunch with her and her husband, but nothing had come of it until now. She and Bev continued their periodic email correspondence until she finally arranged to speak to him on the 'phone and agree to a further meeting.

We were a little disappointed at first when we saw that she had come alone because we were keen to meet other members of the family. However, after a short while Mark, her husband, appeared. He couldn't stay long because he was working and time was short. He was a pleasant, good looking man who appeared younger than his 67 years.

Understandably, introductions were a little awkward but he covered it well with his friendly humour and we were relieved at his attempts to lighten the atmosphere. Then to our delight their daughter, Kelly, also joined us. She was tall and slim with longish red curly hair and we liked her immediately. Well-spoken and articulate she explained how very surprised she had been to learn the secret that her 'Nana' had kept all those years. She was clearly not affected by the revelation as much as her mother, rather more curious than disturbed.

It was interesting to hear her memories of Lilian as a younger woman. Kelly remembered how she had spent quite a lot of time with her because June, her mother, was working. She told us how Lilian would always have little projects for her and her brother like going out for walks and making collections of leaves or fruit in the countryside so that, although they didn't realise it at the time, she was educating as well as amusing them.

She recalled how every Saturday the whole family, including all the cousins, spent time at their grandparents' home. It was the same every week even to the food that they ate which she could still name and she remembered hiding behind the couch when 'Dr Who' was on TV. Lilian clearly loved her family so much that it was hard for Kelly to believe that she would abandon a child to whom she had given birth.

Kelly and June spoke again of how Hector doted on Lilian and how he spoiled her. He would do a lot around the home because she was a busy teacher while he, on the other hand had time for domestic chores. Losing his arm had somewhat blighted his life and taken away his confidence. It was only when June began to learn to play the piano that she discovered that her father could play very well even though he had only one hand.

Conversation eventually turned to Lilian's growing weakness and that led us to reveal our unexpected move to Chicago. We discussed how we might tell Lilian about it and June's immediate response was to say, "Oh I'm having nothing to do with that". However, despite her protestation, she soon began rehearsing what she might say to Lilian to prepare the way for us.

We discussed whether there was a need for us to meet Michael's side of the family but came to the conclusion that, as neither they nor we were asking for a meeting, it could be left since we were pressed for time as we prepared for our move to the USA and, anyway, we planned to be back in the UK periodically so a meeting with them could be arranged to coincide with one of our visits.

This was an enjoyable meeting made easier by Kelly's presence. Being one generation removed from the distressing revelations of the last months, she clearly felt far less emotionally involved and so she helped to keep the conversation objective and engaging. Bev showed them pictures of our family on his camera and Kelly commented, "So these are the cousins that I have never known." We took photos of each other and parted promising to send copies to each other.

Saying goodbye

And so it was that we left England on 1st November 2004 to begin our new life in Chicago. We visited Lilian and met June again before leaving, but simply to say goodbye. Our life in Chicago was hugely demanding, especially for Bev, so I was the one who wrote and sent cards to Lilian and received news of her from June. There was usually little to tell, but distance added enchantment to the view, the correspondence was always welcomed and responses were friendly. We never did visit them again.

Lilian lived on in the nursing home, watched over by her family, until she died on December 11th 2006. She was 96 years old. Her husband, Hector, had died previously aged 98. They had been married for over 70 years.

Part 3
AFTERWARDS

Bev takes up the story

Chapter 40
AFTERWARDS

V al began to receive medical attention soon after our arrival in Chicago, first for displaced discs in her spine which necessitated major surgery, then, just as she emerged from her body brace, she was found to have terminal ovarian cancer. Further invasive surgery prolonged her life for another year.

So we found ourselves, 65 year old strangers far from home, away from our children and grandchildren, early in the process of coming to terms with a new culture, novices struggling to understand a completely different medical system and with our hearts breaking and our minds in turmoil. My new responsibilities in the church were demanding and once again I found myself juggling Val's needs with church responsibilities while trying to stay composed and engaged in business that quickly became almost inconsequential to me in the light of Val's illness and the shortening time we would have together.

The church was wonderfully caring and supportive and within the congregation of some 2000 people we could usually find the skills and experience that we needed to help us to negotiate our way through the

> **Words were so loaded with emotion that they surfaced only with difficulty ...sentences hung in the air unfinished.**

complexities of our new world. We quickly made new friends whose love and companionship proved to be a precious gift of God to us.

Our last Christmas together was marked by an outpouring of love by the church in Chicago. We were overwhelmed by the interest of the congregation so, in order to help people to express their love and prayers for us, we hit on the idea that they might simply give us a small decoration for our Christmas tree. It proved to be an inspired idea! The tree was weighed down with beautiful decorations, each one carefully chosen and many with little messages attached for our encouragement. I still have some of them and as they are brought out each year, I'm reminded of just how precious it is to belong to the family of believers in the Lord Jesus Christ.

Learning the language of separation

When we began to recover our composure from the trauma of first realising the seriousness of Val's condition we made attempts to talk together about what we might expect in the months ahead and to plan for our return to our family in England while Val still had strength for the journey. It was monumentally difficult to put words and thoughts together. We were no strangers to conversations about life and death, it had been a necessary part of our ministry to sit with others and help them to process the stark realities before them, but this conversation was in a category of its own.

I couldn't think straight. Nearly 40 years of pastoral experience seemed to count for very little. Words were so loaded with emotion that they surfaced only with difficulty and sentences hung in the air unfinished. I instinctively felt the need to gain Val's permission to talk about her death and what she wanted me to do for her and after she had gone.

We shadow-boxed for a while but eventually I mentioned a word which she immediately seized on – "afterwards". It became a kind of password which allowed us to talk more freely about the next stage of our life. 'Afterwards' allowed us to look beyond the process of her dying so that we could concentrate more on what awaited her – a better place by far, a sight of the Lord Jesus, an enjoyment of unimaginable glory, freedom from pain, tears, hospitals and chemotherapy! Let's talk about that – and we did!

'Afterwards' for me – meant what? I didn't know. She asked me what I planned to do but I couldn't go there, life was unimaginable without her. Our lives were woven together like a fine tapestry which death would rip apart leaving a thousand ragged ends and broken connections – and me less than half a man.

Many friends from the UK were in contact with us to assure us of their love and prayers for us and one in particular left a lasting impression on us both. I recalled that Dr Steve Brady, Principal of Moorlands College, Christchurch, on the South coast of England, did his doctoral thesis on 'The Intermediate State', that is the Christian theologians' term for the experience of human beings after they die.

What does the Bible teach about those who leave their body to live as spirit beings until the end of the age? Val and I read passages of the Bible and other books on the subject but we still had questions. One day she decided to write to Steve and ask for his help. I have her letter in front of me now as I write. On the 1st January 2006 she wrote,

> *"Suddenly I find myself faced with the most basic questions. Do I really believe the things that I have always said and taught others or are they just an*

intellectual acceptance of a series of doctrines that I have held onto as a means of making sense of the world? I find that as I try to think of the future my knowledge and imagination fail me and it is hard not to look forward with dread. I find that I want to cling to this life.

Why I would want to stay in my body when it is so scarred and uncomfortable, I don't know. But I guess that it is what I am familiar with. The thought of passing through death alone is daunting, of leaving Bev when he has been my friend and constant companion for over 50 years, I must admit that I dread that. How will we experience fellowship with Christ? How will we see Him 'face-to-face' when we are just spirits?"

Steve's reply was more of a pastoral hug than an extract from his thesis. His warmth and understanding was just what we needed. He recalled how our esteemed mutual friend, 'The Doctor', Martyn Lloyd-Jones, received his terminal diagnosis in 1968. He very honestly confessed that he had not reached the Apostles Paul's "desire to be with Christ which is better by far."*

Patiently Steve addressed Val's questions giving us the benefit of his years of study, pointing out that God Himself is Spirit, and He truly lives in ways beyond our imagination. Therefore, we will never be 'just' spirits but will live in ways we can hardly begin to anticipate. Based on Revelation 6:9-11, he wrote of how those who are in spirit with Christ now worship, wonder and wait. Although perfectly happy, they wait patiently for the day of Christ's return and the new heaven and new earth when they will enter their renewed bodies.

Steve concluded his letter with a quote from an American writer, Sara Groves.

"I have a friend who just turned 88
And she just shared that she's afraid of dying.
I sit here years from her experience and try to bring her
comfort.

But what do I know? What do I know?

She grew up singing about the glory land
And she would testify how Jesus changed her life.
It was easy to have faith when she was thirty-four,
But now her friends are dying and death is at her door.
Oh, and what do I know? Really, what do I know?

I don't know if there are harps in heaven
Or the process for earning your wings.
I don't know of bright lights at the end of tunnels
Or any of those things.

She lost her husband after sixty years,
And as he slipped away she still had things to say.
Death can be so inconvenient
You try to live and love
It comes and interrupts.

And what do I know? What do I know?
I don't know if there are harps in heaven.
Or the process for earning your wings.
I don't know of bright lights at the end of tunnels
Or any of those things.

But I know to be absent from the body is to be present
with the Lord
And from what I know of Him, that must be pretty
good.
Oh, I know to be absent from the body is to be present
with the Lord
And from what I know of Him, that must be very
good.""

We returned to the UK in July 2006, to live in the county of Kent, South East England, in a rented house near to our daughter, Kate, and to our son Ian. A hospital and hospice were nearby but Val decided that she wanted to keep further medical intervention to a minimum, no chemotherapy and no doctor's visit unless absolutely necessary. She simply wanted to enjoy her last days quietly with me and enjoy our family as much as she could.

We had three months together before she died on 6th November 2006 aged 66, just over a month before Lilian. We had been married for 44 years. She was in the hospice just one night.

Her Thanksgiving Service was held at The Slade, where we were once again surrounded by a large number of family and friends some of whom had travelled many miles to be with us, three from Chicago.

In the weeks that followed June broke the news of Lilian's death and encouraged me to attend our mother's funeral and meet the extended family. I may have done so but for the fact that Val had died only 5 weeks previously and her funeral had taken place just 2 weeks before Lilian's. I was still buried in my own misery and was relieved to have an important hospital appointment that day.

Christmas with the family was a blur that year and, desolate as I was, I decided nevertheless that I should return to the ice and snow of Chicago in January 2007 and attempt to complete the work we had begun together. It was all I could think of doing – and it proved to be the best decision I could have made at that time.

Despite her weakness, Val worked on the manuscript for 'Somebody's Son' until just a few days before her death when her strength failed. She was determined to complete her gift to us. I read the full story as she had written it for the first time some five months after she had died. Only then could I bring myself to look at it. Then I stored it away.

There is a price to be paid for dysfunctional childhoods. It is paid not only by the children concerned but also by those who get close to them, none more so than their spouse. As I have reflected on our life together I have become increasingly aware of the price Val paid as she walked with me for over 44 years. It was she who bore with my lack of understanding and emotional turmoil. She and Mum Savage, two strong women, affected me deeply by their patient love and were there for me even when I was unable to relate to them as they may have wished.

> There is a price to be paid for dysfunctional childhoods.

Chapter 41
VOCATION AND LOVE

Val and I first met and became friends when
I was still living at Mill Grove. During the
long summer holidays in the early 1950's I
used to go home to stay with Mum and Dad Savage
in Bishopstoke. There were just 6 or 7 of us in the
village church youth club where we met, she with
her bicycle and me on foot. I wanted a bike so much
that I would commandeer hers as often as I could,
sometimes with her sitting on the saddle while I did
the peddling. I recall one memorable occasion when
I unceremoniously tipped her off as we rounded the
corner of Spring Lane to see the formidable figure of
her Gran, a lively Londoner who knew how to speak
her mind, standing at her gate.

This was not the start of the great romance of which
she might have dreamed, and I have to confess that
I probably thought as much about her bike as I did
of her at first. But I was beginning to discover girls
and enjoyed her company so when I returned to
Mill Grove after the holidays were over I boasted to
my friends that I had a girlfriend 'back home'. She
would probably have been very surprised to hear me
say that!

So we were already friends when I returned

Do you want a man like that?

permanently to the village in the summer of 1955 and I soon got to know her very well as we spent an increasing amount of time together. Our friendship grew almost imperceptibly into love for each other over the ensuing years although her parents were not at all happy about it.

An unsuitable liaison!

They knew Ted Foderingham and his reputation since he did his house calls in their area - and they eventually learned from Val that I was his child. She felt compelled to tell them because previously they only knew that I had come from a childrens' home and understandably that added a significant element of risk to her getting too involved with me, let alone marrying me. Val thought that if they knew who my father was, they would be more agreeable to our relationship, but it was not to be. As Ted Foderingham's son they were firmly of the opinion that I would follow in his footsteps. "He's likely to turn out to behave like his father. Do you want a man like that?" they said. "You are blinded by what you think is love."

They could well have been right, of course, but Val was convinced that they were wrong. She tried to explain to them that she believed that the power of God had changed me but they had little time for such talk and used my background to further ridicule her and her faith.

Sadly, our wedding day was not the happiest day of our lives. I can see Val now settling into the railway carriage as it pulled out of Eastleigh station and saying with huge relief, "Oh! It's over! I'm free!"

Her parents remained pretty hostile to me until some years after we were married but, having witnessed how we came through Val's illness together, they eventually came to accept me even though we were never close.

From the time I first professed faith in the Lord Jesus Christ I had a clear sense of vocation. I can't explain it but I just knew that I wanted to be a Christian Minister. Val would have much preferred me to become a teacher but there was never any question in my mind that, if we were to be married, she would need to accept that one day she would become the wife of a minister, or maybe a missionary.

Educational frustrations

One of the great regrets of my life has always been that, because of the circumstances of my early years, my education was badly neglected. I started school late because of illness and missed out altogether on taking the eleven plus examination that could have led to a Grammar School place because at the time I was moving from Bishopstoke to Tiptree.

I have no recollection of how I did at school in Tiptree but the records from St Barnabas Secondary Modern School in Woodford show that, although I came top in my 'C' stream classes three years running, I was not moved to the more demanding 'B' stream. The reasons for that are not clear but the effect was to leave me frustrated at my lack of education.

I've felt that I've never caught up with those whose schooling was uninterrupted. I left school just a few weeks before my fifteenth birthday with no qualifications and began my working life, as did most of the boys in Eastleigh at that time, first as an office boy and then as an apprentice in the locomotive workshops of British Railways Southern Region.

Despite this, my sense of vocation increased and I only ever viewed my time in industry as a necessary stepping stone to get where I longed to be.

I questioned every visiting minister that Mum and Dad Savage entertained in their home on Sundays and found out from them what I would need to do to gain entry into college.

I would leave for work at 6.45am each morning and return home at 5pm. Sometimes Val and I would pass each other on our bicycles during the lunch break as she cycled home from Eastleigh Grammar School in her green uniform and white ankle socks while I, called back to work by the powerful hooter that boomed across the town and the surrounding countryside, headed to the factory in my dirty overalls and steel capped boots.

In the evenings, after a quick meal and change of clothes, I would head out again for classes in the school that Val inhabited during the day so that little by little, over a period of several years, I gained the basic qualifications necessary to prepare me for Theological College.

The single motivation for my solitary devotion to learning was the compelling sense of calling to ministry but, even when armed with the necessary qualifications, there were some in the church who thought that I would be best advised to stay put in the factory. They knew where I came from and no doubt could see how much I needed to develop if I was to become suitable for such a calling. Our own minister at the time warned Val that, even if I was to be accepted by a college she, with her Grammar school education, would need to give me significant support if I was to succeed, so she prepared herself to help me as much as she could for the challenges ahead - and challenges there were for both of us.

Our courtship was abruptly interrupted when, at eighteen years of age, Val left grammar school and headed off to the South Coast resort of Weymouth, some sixty miles away, to train as a teacher, returning two years later to join the staff of the village primary school in which she herself had once been a pupil.

It took just a few months after her return for us to decide finally that we were meant to be together for the rest of our lives and I slipped an engagement ring on her finger early one spring Sunday morning in 1960 down beside the river that ran through the meadows at the bottom of the village, one of our favourite haunts. Later that day the entire church celebrated our engagement with us.

We talked often about what our married life would be like and of my conviction that I should become a Minister. I did not qualify for a grant for my training but I had saved a little money from my meagre wages, and so we decided that we would not take up a mortgage and buy a house as many did when they married, instead we would buy a residential caravan which we could sell when the time came, using the proceeds to pay the fees for my first year in college. I would continue to a second and third year only if funds became available for me to do so. If it really was God who was calling me to the ministry, he would supply our needs.

If the money was not there, we would take it that our friends were right and I would return to work at the lathe and the bench. There was no shame in that but there was no disguising the fact that I would be devastated if that happened.

We were married in Bishopstoke Evangelical Church on 4th August 1962 and began our married life in a large static caravan located in the beautiful Hampshire countryside a mile outside the village. We loved it! However, winter that year was one of the coldest and most prolonged on record.

Known as the 'Big Freeze', temperatures in Britain plummeted and lakes and rivers froze over. Nothing moved on the canals for months and this in large measure led to the transfer of freight from barge to rail, and eventually to road. At the end of December a blizzard swept across South West England and Wales. Snow drifted to over 20 feet deep in places, driven on by gale force easterly winds, blocking roads and railways.

January 1963 was the coldest month of the twentieth century, indeed the coldest since January 1814. We woke each morning to find that our breath had condensed on the walls of the caravan and had turned to ice and even the liquid gas that supplied us with heat and hot water froze in its bottles. We huddled for warmth in our ice box saved from freezing completely by an electric blanket. We were triumphant that we were among the last survivors to leave the caravan park, but eventually we too submitted to the inevitable and moved out until spring came.

College at last

It was 1964 before the opportunity came at last for me to enrol as a student in South Wales Bible College. By then Val had left teaching to care for our first child, Philip. Our financial resources were, as predicted, entirely inadequate for what we planned. So we were grateful to accept the invitation of Victor and Margaret White for Val to join the staff at Mill Grove and for her and Philip, our bouncing six month old, to live in the Home in South Woodford while I studied in South Wales. In this way Val would continue to care for Philip while working in the Home in exchange for accommodation and support and our savings would be released to pay for my fees.

It was a generous provision but very much harder than we expected for us to live almost 300 miles apart from each other after only two years of married life and with our first baby so young. But we comforted ourselves with the thought that we would be separated only during term times and the course might only last for one year if funds ran out.

In the event the arrangement did last for only one year, but not principally because of lack of finance. It is true that we had very little income, but the main reason for Val and Philip to leave Mill Grove and join me in South Wales was that I couldn't bear to be separated from them.

We agonised over the decision for weeks but there was nothing for it; if I was to complete my training, Val would need to be alongside me. Victor White, the Director of Mill Grove, seemed to understand my need. He had been separated from his wife, Margaret, for over four years during the second world war. He explained to Val that now I had a family of my own at last, losing it after so short a time was far too stressful to sustain.

It remains a mystery how we survived the practical and financial demands of the two final years of my training but we did, and we learned valuable lessons in the process. Living in Mill Grove provided unforgettable examples to us both of what it means to exercise faith in the God who cares for his children in the most detailed way.

Ian, our second son was born in October 1966 and in the summer of 1967 I successfully completed the three year diploma course with a distinction in Systematic Theology and emerged from college to take up temporary employment as a ward orderly in a local hospital that specialised in treating Welsh miners. Again it proved to be an invaluable experience since I gradually learned to overcome my aversion to all things medical and prepare for a lifetime of visiting dozens of hospitals and hundreds of sick and dying people.

In the spring of 1968 I was invited to become the Minister of Donnington Evangelical Church in Willesden, North West London, and believing this to be God's will for us, we moved back to London, a prospect that Val found very daunting and unattractive. But there was never any question that, whatever the cost, she would do what we both believed to be God's will.

Chapter 42

TRAUMA!

The congregation of thirty met in a small chapel in Donnington Road. It had been built many years earlier in the garden of one of its former members and, although it had employed ministers before me, I was the first one to serve the people full-time in over thirteen years.

The members alone were responsible for housing and paying its minister so it was a huge undertaking for them to employ a penniless novice pastor, his wife and two children. But they rose to the challenge, purchased a two bedroomed ground floor maisonette near to the church and provided us with a regular income which was small but sacrificially given.

In the apartment above us lived an elderly couple with whom we attempted to make friends but the presence of our two young children was too much for them and from the outset they seemed determined to make our lives difficult.

The first few months of being a Christian minister I found daunting, to say the least. Being a small church there was no senior minister to tell me how to manage my time or set priorities for what I would do each day. In common with many small missions and chapels in central London and its inner suburbs,

> **Each looked at the other as though they had just seen aliens performing some strange ritual.**

Donnington Church was supported by members who, having grown more affluent, had moved out to leafier and smarter areas. It was their ongoing interest and generosity that provided the means by which the church survived and had the resources to employ us.

However, over the years there had been enormous changes in the area they had left behind and, without realising it, they had gradually lost touch with its people and culture.

As a minister it fell to me to work each day within the multi-cultural community of local residents while also serving the largely white middle class long-standing members of the church who drove like visiting missionaries to Sunday services and midweek meetings. Most decisions were made by them and any initiatives that came from the local people had to pass muster with them.

The difference between these two groups of people was illustrated rather humorously on one occasion when the church held a social event at which the daughter of one family played the violin to great applause from those who had watched her grow up. She was closely followed by a group of West Indian lads from my newly formed youth club who gyrated to recently released reggae music. Each looked at the other as though they had just seen aliens performing some strange ritual.

College had trained me to think and to explain the Bible, but it had done little to prepare me to manage the practicalities of church life. Overnight I became responsible for almost everything that happened in the church. It felt a lonely task since the most experienced and influential members were not readily on hand to advise me as I tackled the issues of daily ministry life. They were understandably absorbed in their demanding professional responsibilities travelling in and out of central London each day.

No matter that the congregation was small, there were still necessary administrative tasks to attend to and the unremitting demand to prepare at least three main teaching sessions each week, two Sunday sermons and one midweek Bible study. They needed to be sufficiently nutritious to feed the statistician, the surveyor and the professor, the chemist, teachers and artists who attended Sunday services but also accessible to those who were less able. In addition there was the youth club to run, the elderly to care for and a few weddings and funerals to conduct.

I still recall how devastated I was when the local carpenter and his wife came to tell me that they would be leaving the church to attend another nearby. "We just don't fit here", they said. "We know that you do your best but the people in the church are not really like us and our friends. We feel embarrassed to invite them to come along because they won't fit in." If they did not feel at home in the church, what hope would there be for its future and how was I to bridge the gap between the two very different communities?

The workload was not unexpected, of course, but before long I was feeling the strain. I needed no one to encourage me to work, for this appointment was a dream come true for me and I entered into the role enthusiastically. But, since there was no one to tell me when to stop working or to remind me to balance the demands of my new life with my primary responsibility to care for my family, I worked longer days than was probably necessary and was often away from home.

Val would gently remind me of family events but, since she knew how demanding I found the work and was keen to support me, she quietly

I woke up to find that I hardly knew Val anymore.

took on responsibility for nearly all our domestic arrangements.

Now, in common with many ministers with whom I have spoken over the years, I look back with huge regret for being slow to notice that she also was becoming overwhelmed as she tried to make ends meet and care for the family and, in addition, cope with the increasingly oppressive presence of our elderly neighbours above us.

The congregation was patient with us and supported us and soon new people were attracted to the church so that the building was often quite full. Income began to rise so we updated the inside of the church building and increased its activities.

And our family also grew with Kathryn Jane's arrival in December 1969. She was soon to be renamed 'Kate' and 'golden nugget' by the boys. "A girl to complete your family", members said knowingly, scarcely disguising their sincere hope that we would stop producing more mouths to feed.

Life changed forever

Then one day, five years into our time in Willesden, I woke up to find that I hardly knew Val anymore. She suddenly became uncontrollably active and sleepless. Neither of us slept for four nights.

Normally reticent about taking on new things, her imagination began to work overtime and nothing seemed impossible for her to accomplish. The world became a wonderful place, full of light and colour and people full of love. Caution was thrown to the wind and normal routines were abandoned.

The children, sensing that something was wrong, began to be alarmed and I was caught between caring for them and trying to calm Val without success.

At last, and with great reluctance, I called for help

and a psychiatrist was sent to our home. She took little time to confirm that Val was suffering from complete exhaustion and from some form of mental illness. She needed to be hospitalised immediately.

I was stunned. There was no history of mental ill health in her family. We had always thought of her as the most resilient one in our marriage and most prepared for life's challenges. She came from a relatively stable home even if her parents were unsympathetic to her faith, and she was well educated and appeared strong. I was the one who was less well equipped to cope with life and needed support, so others said, and so we believed. No wonder I was so reluctant to act on what I saw and heard from her.

And so began four years of travelling between doctors and hospitals for consultations and in-patient care.

Treatment appeared to consist mainly of experimentation with powerful drugs in a search to discover which ones most suited Val's condition. Several drugs had alarming side effects and one left her fearing for her life.

In addition to my anxieties about Val I was constantly preoccupied with the needs of the children, making sure that I spent time with them, trying my hand at cooking and making endless arrangements for other people to transport them to and from their functions and care for them when I needed to be elsewhere. Church members were distressed by the turmoil that engulfed our family and supported us as much as they could and it was their practical help and kindness that enabled us to get through each day.

I gradually developed a routine for juggling school attendance and holidays, hospital visits, sermon preparation and pastoral visiting. Amazingly, people said that my preaching improved during this period although how that came to be I have little idea. Maybe their sympathy for our predicament made them more sympathetic and receptive and undoubtedly their prayers for us brought God's grace to us.

Thankfully we were able to remain together as a family through what seemed to be an unrelenting, very dark and testing experience that engulfed and threatened to overwhelm us.

Some months into her illness, Dr Martyn Lloyd-Jones visited our home. Not only was he a world-renowned theologian and preacher, he was also a highly respected and accomplished medical doctor and, since I was a member of the Westminster Fellowship, a gathering of ministers from across the United Kingdom who met each month under his chairmanship, he took a particular interest in us.

Had he known that I was also a former family member of Mill Grove, his interest may have been even more intense but as it was he could hardly have been more generous.

'The Doctor', was thorough in examining every detail of what had led to Val's illness eventually making arrangements for us to meet a Christian psychiatrist who was experimenting with a new regime of drugs at that time. For Val to be given the high dosage that he recommended she needed to be under constant supervision and, since he worked in a long stay mental institution some distance from our home, it became necessary to admit her.

In the weeks that followed, I sometimes had no alternative but to drive to Friern Barnet Hospital in North London with the children and leave them locked in the car while I made my way through labyrinthine passages to find her in a cheerless room staring into space. Residents wandered the grounds, some behaving strangely, while our three watched them nervously from within the car, fearing for their safety.

For all the turmoil that swamped us as a family, nothing compared to the severity and intensity of Val's suffering.

We never forgot the experience of entering that vast, grim Victorian Asylum for the first time along whose endless corridors shuffled the broken minded. We felt as though we had travelled back in time to something much darker, more primitive and far less friendly than what we experienced at our local hospital psychiatric unit.

Many years later Val wrote very movingly of her illness and of her experience of that institution. What follows is her recollection of that time. A similar account was published in 'Professional Nurse' in February 1992.

Chapter 43

IN AND OUT OF
THE SHADOWS -
VAL'S REFLECTIONS

Tediously, pointlessly I ask myself over and over,
'What am I doing here? What am I doing here
watching this unremarkable drama?' They say the
story goes back to my childhood. They say perhaps to the
womb. I answer wearily the many silly questions from
many different faces in many different rooms. As far as
I can tell it goes back ten months or so only. Before that I
considered myself so ordinary, normal, totally predictable,
a boring mother of three boisterous, laughing, squabbling,
questioning youngsters – yet locked into myself, alienated.

A village girl unable to adapt to the brittle tensions of
a north-west London multi-racial community – rather
many different communities living uneasily alongside
one another – and I could find my place in none of them.
The drab, lonely loveless streets did not receive me and
indoors there was no respite. For there I was oppressed
and fatigued beyond measure by the invisible yet all-
pervading presence of the elderly couple above us with
their slammings of doors and hammerings on floors, futile
protests at the noise of the children.

One day, inevitably so it seems now, a thick, tight
constricting band suddenly released inside me. I walked

out into the June sunshine with my husband. Hand in hand we walked across the park just to collect our little girl from nursery but for me it was a stroll through Paradise. As if we were in some corny movie the sun had never seemed so brilliant, the June roses so sweetly fragrant. Passers-by had the faces of angels and I wanted to smile and smile and tell them all that I loved them.

The next days were a rising falling roller-coaster of exciting fantasies. Life was so good, so full of endless possibilities, a fast-moving kaleidoscope of disconnected, colourful memories and unformed dreams for the future. Sleep became rare. Who wants to sleep when there was so much to do, to plan, to talk about? Housework and children forgotten, my pen flew faster and faster as I vainly tried to record my dreams.

Gathering momentum, higher and higher, faster and faster the swing flew, soaring up into hitherto unknown realms of expectation and pleasure. At last I was really alive! Below me, dimly, I caught glimpses of the anxious faces of friends and family, alarmed, even angry - "Sit down, sit down, SIT DOWN YOU'RE ROCKING THE BOAT", they shouted but I could hardly hear them. Irritated by their concern I laughed and pushed myself higher.

'It's my party and I'll laugh if I want to!'

Then, inevitably, the swing went out of control. Dizzy, confused I was tossed into the ether in a wide terrifying arc. No longer was my mind able to form into any reasonable, recognisable pattern from the multitude of memories, thoughts, plans that were raining down on me like thousands and thousands of unrelated jig-saw puzzle pieces. Desperately, night and day I ran round and round like a hot sticky child triumphantly fixing together odd pieces here and there. But where have I put those other pieces?

Inwardly I cried out, demented. The swing had catapulted right over the bar to crash down, juddering to a standstill, jarring every nerve and bone.

Now, there was an empty stillness, a void, every sensation, every emotion stilled, though not quite. It was more as though some deceitful hand had quietly, finally switched off the power and plunged into darkness one half of my brain. A slow miserable symphony played but with no lilting soprano refrains. I could hear only the slow, melancholy groan of a monotonous bass line.

There was no pleasure in my days, no joy, no anticipation of happiness to come. Dark emotions ruled completely, dread, anxiety, panic, foreboding. One moment trapped in a lake of frozen anger, the next sucked helplessly down and down into a slimy, suffocating pit of desolation. Far above, beyond my reach, I watched the life of my husband and children going on seemingly as normal without me. I peered at them as through the far end of a telescope but could not reach them. Finally, apathy made me no longer even want to. I sat motionless in the dark watching without interest the flickering screen of other peoples' lives playing out before me.

And was that you my Father so far, far away in the distance? Did you really have your back so firmly turned against me? It seemed so. Ancient of Days were you deaf to your daughter's sobs? Even your Beloved protested at such a thing. His cry of dereliction became mine. "My God, my God why hast Thou forsaken me? Why art Thou so far from helping me, and from the words of my roaring?"

The next months are just a dim recalling of consultations, questions and swallowed pills, downers, uppers, sleepers changed every ten days or so. Then yet more pills to counteract the side-effects of the first. I was so cold, shivering, shaking, trembling, dry-mouthed, hiding away in bathrooms and bedrooms, sobbing uncontrollably, hoping no-one would hear. Longing to sleep to block it all out, to sleep perhaps never to wake?

I walked with my husband one day in the park. Our four year old strode out in front of me her head held high. She walked with the assured confidence of one who seems to know that she is beautiful, of one who is constantly admired and glanced at. Her strawberry blonde hair bobbed and glowed in the autumn sunshine. She turned back to me, her plump cheeks and eyes so full of vibrancy and colour. "Come on, Mum", she called to the bowed colourless figure behind her, "don't look so sad".

'It's your party, young one, have fun, you have to
But I'll cry, I just need to'

The months crawled by, each second a minute, each minute a dragging hour. Christmas came and went unnoticed. It must have been early April when we walked in Kew Gardens. We had an elderly friend with us who, with his usual warm exuberance, my husband had gently persuaded into a wheelchair. She had been imprisoned in her flat all winter, confined by the limits of painful arthritis, but now, self-consciousness forgotten, she was gazing at the resurrection freshness of that April day with ecstasy. She looked and looked with hungry eyes, exclaiming with delight over every detail of the panorama before her. I looked too but my eyes relished nothing. I was still in the grip of winter ice and darkness. She was very old, a widow enduring pain alone each long day. I was young and healthy, cushioned around with friends and family. She was contented and delighted that day while I outwardly apathetic, was inwardly distraught and screaming.

'It's your party, old one, enjoy it, your last one,
but I'll cry I just have to'

By the end of April I was admitted to a hospital in North London, a vast, grim Victorian building – but these were not Victorian times. This was 1975.

I sat with my husband and Mr. Brigston, Consultant Psychiatrist, as they discussed what should be done. In silence I listened appalled. How had it come to this? Last night a friend had called:

> *'Oh, do come in. I'm all alone.*
> *I got your message on the phone.*
> *You've come to help? That's great.*
> *Something particular to say? Oh, well then fire away.'*

But she filled my reluctant yet fascinated ears with graphic details. Evil spirits, she said had dominated and possessed her but they had all one by one been cast out. With shrieks and screams she had vomited them out, a foul stream, green and wriggling worms, black slimy snakes, out they had come. She was released and freed. Of course, that's it. I too must be inhabited by demons. Of course this must be the root of my sickness.

I could not fail to grasp the implication of what she said but the effect on my already wounded mind was devastating. Pressing on heavily with a little housework the next day I found myself time and again glancing over my shoulder, alert, alarmed at the fleeting sense of another presence in the flat. Nothing, of course, was to be seen.

I could take no more and so it was that the two men with great concern were deciding that I would have to be admitted that day. I said nothing – "As a sheep before her shearers is dumb ..." From across the little room I heard his voice say in distress, "I really can't cope with the children and my wife as well". I said nothing. Drugs paralysed thoughts and words but also I knew that what he said was true. There was no point in arguing. If they had asked me I would have shrugged my shoulders and said nothing. Yet secretly I was so grieved that such a decision should be made for me.

Driving home to pack a few things we passed our

children's school. Seeing the car, our eldest son ran to the wire fencing. Flushed and excited from play, he called to us, dark bright eyes, crooked-toothed grin. My husband jumped out to talk to the boy. I watched listlessly from the car. The silent conversation between father and son brought a change to his face, fear spreading its shade. I did nothing to comfort him, just waved as we drove away, choking and gagging on misery. He clung onto the wire and watched us go.

> *'No son, you can't come in to me.*
> *Go off and play, you'll soon forget, be free.*
> *It's me behind the wire not you, it's me'*

"Do you know your name? When were you born? Do you remember? Do you know what day it is today?" He asked the questions, his voice casual, cold even. I tried to understand. I did understand the necessity for such questions yet still it hurt. Pride whines pathetically when it is slashed even a little at its roots. But was it really necessary for me to strip off until nearly naked to be examined and why was the door left wide open for a procession of people to walk by and glance in?

> *'Oh do come in, feel free,*
> *No please, please don't mind me.'*

No-one welcomed me onto the ward, no-one said a word, no rules or routine were explained. I did just what everyone else did, sat in silence in the day room watching with fear the other patients. An old lady wandering from chair to chair, standing by each of us in turn, just staring and staring; a dishevelled man pacing up and down indecently uncovered by ill-fitting pyjamas – "don't be a nuisance old chap, just sit down and watch the tele". A tiny twig-like lady shaking violently as she lit cigarette after cigarette.

I heard words: 'paranoid, schizophrenic, psychotic, manic, neurotic, psychopathic, alcoholic, ECT! I had only the vaguest notion of their meanings but they brought such terror. Someone said, "I've been here six years now." A mournful Irish voice complained, "Oi'm bored and Oi'm lonely." What am I doing here with these poor people? It's a terrible mistake. I shouldn't be here.

I rushed into the room where my things had been put and fell on the bed, a pathetic heap of hysterical weeping. "Now then, just stop that, don't be so silly! You must come out into the day room. You must not stay in here. I've just come all the way from Malaysia. I'm lonely too but I'm not crying am I?"

'Oh you've come in, how nice.
Yes, I'm sure I need your professional advice.
You're young but trained, an expert for sure.
Yes, those other patients they're my cure.'

I followed her out meekly but no-one looked up, no-one spoke. Only the TV in the corner paid me any attention. It screamed and shouted at me. A frocked cleric was gripping a man by the shoulders, exorcising his devils. The tormented soul fell to the ground, smitten, screeching, shaking with violent spasms. A strange coincidence, or was there really some minor demon with a warped humour enjoying this cruel joke?

I'll have a bath. I'll find a place of refuge, a place to escape, I thought. But there was no way to lock the door. I'll just have to be quick and hope for the best. Yet hardly had I stepped into the water when a male nurse, certainly my junior, marched in. Standing close to the edge of the bath he looked down at me irritated, apparently astonished. "Do you usually take a bath so late?", he demanded, "It's half-past eight". Duly shamed and embarrassed I mumbled some excuse for my outrageous behaviour.

'Oh Hi! Come on in. Have we met?
So sorry, I seem to be rather wet!'

I was thankful for a single room but every few minutes the door would fly open and a voice, male or female, would call indifferently "Good morning. Are you getting up? Are you all right?" before moving quickly on. I resorted to propping open the wardrobe door and skulking behind it to dress as quickly as my mind and hands would allow.

'Come in, don't bother to knock.
Shall I wear these jeans or that old frock?'

Faces appeared frequently in the glass window in the door –

'Oh Hi, do look in sometime, come in for a chat,
It would be nice, I'd really like that.'

There was only one, a gentle Asian lad named Danny, who talked to me once or twice. He sat beside me and asked me what I was reading and had I ever been a teacher? "You shouldn't be here. This isn't the right place for you", he said. I drank his words thirstily, at least one person saw, one person knew.

The sister on the ward spoke twice to me that month. "It's against the rules", she said briskly, removing our children's pictures and letters. They were fastened to that window in the door to block out the sleep-disturbing light. Well, you've got to have rules haven't you?

The second time she shouted to me across the large dining room as I walked through. "How did you come to have a breakdown?" Really interested she was. But did she truly imagine that I would call cheerfully back to her before listening ears and watching eyes? Could I really confide in one brief shouted sentence the whole course of my life? I felt so tired; walking on I called back over my shoulder in exasperation, "I really don't know!"

'You want to come in? But did I invite you, I don't recall?
Well, gate-crash my life, I don't mind at all.'

Together we walked in the beautiful grounds in those first days, my husband somehow already a stranger from my other world. Together we watched the bizarre behaviour of other patients – a man marching in strict time with himself, roaring sergeant-major style commands, another laughing aloud at some wonderful secret joke. And worst of all, emerging from locked wards, little lines of long-forgotten ghosts. Hands linked they shuffled, zombies leaving puddles behind them. Men relieved themselves behind wooden screens, leering and whistling over the top as we passed.

I thought of other hospitals like this around London and multiplied their number as I remembered all the other cities in Britain. Eventually my imagination added on every city of every country on earth. The vast number of broken people stretched to infinity, too many to count.

'Yes, come in with me, come in and see.
But please, please take me home, don't leave me.'

I cried on his shoulder, sad for them now more than for me.

Yet, amazingly, after four or five days I calmed and settled. I reasoned with myself, what is there to be afraid of? All they do is hand you medication. They're not going to operate on your brain. At least you don't have to make decisions in here. Why not just rest and accept the situation?'

'I came into that place just to see
Yet quickly its doors almost closed on me.'

A private solitary routine of listening to the radio, reading book after book and walking in the grounds had taken shape when quite suddenly it seemed I was told, "You can go home this afternoon."

Was Lazarus alarmed and reluctant when commanded with a shout to live? Did he cling for a moment to the familiar shadowy world of Sheol? But the voice was clear and certain, "Lazarus, come forth!" He must live, and I too must rise. I must live again in that world from which I had retreated for so long. I stumbled out, blinking uncertainly in the strong light. The shadows released me but it would be many, many months before I could completely throw off the clinging grave clothes that had bound me for so long. Two or was it three years passed before I walked in crisp autumn woods with the wind on my face and heard myself saying simply, "I've enjoyed this afternoon."

Chapter 44

HOME AGAIN

It was a relief to have Val home again but we were under no illusion that her illness was at an end. I prepared the children for her return as much as I could but there was no denying the pain that her shuffling presence brought to us all.

They were alarmed at first but little by little we adjusted and she fought her way back to taking up her life in the family again. Our faithful band of helpers gradually relaxed and withdrew and in time we learned to come to terms with a new normal way of life as we all recovered from the trauma of those years.

I cannot think of Val's suffering without a deep love and admiration for her courage and determination to go on believing that her Heavenly Father would come to deliver her whether in life or in death. Many years later we talked together of her fight with the temptation to take her own life. It was real and very tempting but, such was her deep conviction that she was a child of God and her care was in His hands, that she just couldn't bring herself to do it. To kill herself would mean that she would stand before Him to give an account of her action and that was more daunting to her than enduring her terrible suffering. Had he not promised, "My grace is sufficient for you, for my power is made perfect in weakness"?*

Then she must believe Him even though everything in her experience at that time seemed to deny the reality of His care for her.

I can still hear her praying using words from James Montgomery's classic hymn which begins, "According to Thy gracious word", words that expressed her deepest desire. If ever again she lost control of her mental faculties, all she asked was that she would never be forgotten or abandoned by her Lord! The full verse says,

> "And when these failing lips grow dumb
> And mind and memory flee,
> When Thou shalt in Thy kingdom come,
> Jesus, remember me."

She reduced the words simply to,

> "When mind and memory flee,
> Jesus, remember me."

Many who knew Val in the years following her illnesses will remember her as somewhat withdrawn, vulnerable, even a lonely figure who lived quietly behind my shadow. To me, however, she will always be someone whom I loved, admired and valued more than I can possibly say. She taught me what true godliness is. She demonstrated Christ's power to keep his children in their deepest afflictions and most tortuous trials.

Only since her death have I discovered the song made famous by Bette Midler, "The Wind Beneath My Wings". The Bible describes the Holy Spirit as being like the wind who comes alongside believers to help them fly. Neither I, nor Val, would have been anything without Him, but I can't help it, the lyrics always remind me of her.

"It must have been cold there in my shadow,
To never have sunlight on your face.
You were content to let me shine, that's your way.
You always walked a step behind.

So I was the one with all the glory,
While you were the one with all the strength.
A beautiful face without a name for so long.
A beautiful smile to hide the pain.
Did you ever know that you're my hero,
And everything I would like to be?

It might have appeared to go unnoticed,
But I've got it all here in my heart.
I want you to know I know the truth, of course I know it.
I would be nothing without you.
Did you ever know that you're my hero?
You're everything I wish I could be.
I can fly higher than an eagle,
For you are the wind beneath my wings."

Our family was never quite the same again after her illness but we had more than survived the experience. We had grown very close through our shared pain and I had learned to watch over Val and the children much more carefully. We also came to appreciate the family of Christian believers so much. Their prayers and sacrificial service made it possible for us to cope and probably kept our children from following where their father had once gone, into care – maybe into Mill Grove. At least they would have been safe and loved there.

Chapter 45
THE SINS OF THE FATHERS

I suppose that, with the increasing inclination in older years to reflect more on the course of one's life, it was inevitable that I would return eventually to ponder what happened to cause Val's illness, to examine how we handled it and the lifetime of clouds that hung over us to the end. I wonder if the difficulties of my early years affected my ability to understand what she was going through and my capacity to support and protect her. Can I ever know the answer to that question with any certainty?

People observe my deficits, no doubt, as I observe their privileges, but it is impossible to identify conclusively the impact of our formative years on the course of our life. I can only offer my impression of their effect on my life but hasten to add that my experience, although it may resonate with others from similar backgrounds, is no yardstick by which to judge what they may expect. Each person's childhood leaves them with a unique legacy, both positive and negative.

I have noticed that it is common for those of us who were denied a regular family in a stable home to imagine that living with mum and dad and brothers

> A poor start in life can leave wounds that may be deeply buried and largely unknown to those who carry them.

and sisters, and having aunts and uncles in the wings, must be bliss. However, that is self-evidently not the case. The reality is that regular family life has problems of its own and it is not uncommon to hear people say that they couldn't wait to get away from their family because of the damaging behaviour of their parents or siblings, or simply because they just didn't get along with each other. That's a simple fact of life in this broken world.

The importance of family

So the elevation of close family in the imaginations of those of us who never enjoyed it is likely to have more to do with our own profound need to belong and to be special to someone. There is evidently something about filial relationships that nothing else can quite replicate or replace.

Well into adult life I was suddenly ambushed by an upsurge of emotion and misery when I read that my father denied that I belonged to him. Where did that come from? Why did it matter so much? How could I possibly care about the opinion of a man who neglected and rejected me 60 years earlier?

I can only conclude that a poor start in life can leave wounds that may be deeply buried and largely unknown to those who carry them.

In stable and loving families, nesting parents and fascinated grandparents prepare for the arrival of a child long before it is born. As they are cuddled and cosseted from infancy to puberty and beyond, their children enjoy a security that, unbeknown to them, provides an underlying sense of their value and feeds their confidence. They learn to understand themselves in the context of the family, to love what their parents and grandparents love and absorb family values and traditions seamlessly. The influence and affirmation of the family is woven into their very being.

But it is not so for us. We find ourselves starting late and trying to pick things up as we go along – and we never seem to quite catch up. We search for affirmation from people around us and are left to make our own assessment of what is good for us and what is harmful and youthful immaturity and ignorance of the world often leads to poor choices and damaging outcomes.

I was blessed to be taken in by two loving and supportive substitute families. Their care, and their enjoyment of a Higher Love, lessened my deficit significantly. Above all, my own lifelong enjoyment of Christ and His love has saved me from much that is damaging and has provided sufficient security for me to take risks in reaching out and becoming vulnerable to other people.

But it still mattered that my father denied that I belonged to him. I remain puzzled by that and, since I made the discovery, I've wondered what else remains hidden that continues to affect my life.

I hope that few will be aware of it but I have always found it a challenge to sustain close, meaningful relationships. They have usually come about because other people persisted in getting to know me.

Without even being aware of it, I seemed to have chosen early in life to live in my own internal world and interact with other people only cautiously if at all, somewhat like the Miller of Dee whose song I remember from childhood,

"I live by my mill, God bless her! She's kindred, child, and wife;
I would not change my station for any other in life;
No lawyer, surgeon, or doctor e'er had a groat from me;
I care for nobody, no not I if nobody cares for me."

It took me some time to learn what a barren and crippling outlook that is, for, as others have wisely commented, we know nothing as we should, not even ourselves, if we live in isolation. We need people around us to teach us, correct us, to bring perspective to our joys and sorrows and share their life lessons with us. I could have learned so much more from those who walked with me even briefly over the years had I been less self-contained and I could have given more of myself to them.

Happily, despite the acute stress of Val's illness, our love deepened and our marriage did more than survive the trauma. The grace of God protected and blessed us. Our children have gone on to do very well in life and to raise their children with love and care. They bring me great joy in my older years and for that I am increasingly thankful.

Chapter 46
COLOURFUL CANVAS

A s family life returned to a more regular pattern and the hospital visits became less frequent, we began to consider whether it might be time to move on from the church in Willesden. We had new friendly neighbours upstairs and felt greatly indebted to those who had stood by us through Val's illness but our family had outgrown the two bedroomed maisonette and we all needed a fresh start.

We had been ten years in Willesden, a long period in a first church, but we couldn't move earlier. Even now it was not the best time to move the children. Philip 14, Ian 11 and Kate 8 faced upheaval and disruption to their education but there was nothing for it, for their sakes as well ours, if an invitation came to us to move elsewhere, we agreed that we would consider it positively.

And one day it did, without any prompting on our part.

In November 1977, I was invited to preach at a church in Plumstead Common, South East London. At first, the idea that this could be our next assignment was unattractive to us both. We had hoped for a quieter, more rural location outside of

London but we soon discovered that, despite its London postcode, it was an attractive area with a large open common and a rural feel to its landscape. Estate agents called it 'the North Kent borders' making it sound far more attractive than 'London SE18'.

We returned to the church several times before the members finally invited us to join its leadership and each time we came away a little more certain that we should accept, at least I did. Understandably, Val took a while longer to reach the same conclusion.

The church was much larger than we had previously experienced and its building was situated in the heart of the long established suburban community. Most of the people lived close by and their friendliness won us over.

On the day that Dr Martyn Lloyd-Jones preached at our introductory service, he assured Val privately that he thought she would be very happy there. And so it proved to be – at least as far as her ongoing condition allowed.

The Slade Evangelical Church, so called because of the road in which it is set, sits high up on the north side of Shooters Hill, a landmark in South East London. It has commanding views over a small ravine and the town of Plumstead below which borders a low lying marshland that drains into the Thames.

The church has a rich and colourful history dating back to the 1870's and once boasted a Sunday School with over five hundred children. By the time we arrived in 1978 the numbers were far smaller than 100 years earlier but still over two hundred adults attended Sunday services and a sizeable Boys Brigade and Girls Brigade with a marching band proudly paraded through the streets each month.

The church was full of London characters. As older

members of the congregation related their history to us we noted the recurring theme that they had 'come from across the river', sounding rather like Jews who had escaped slavery in Egypt. In fact they had been evacuated south of London's river Thames because heavy bombing in the Second World War targeted and destroyed the docklands and the surrounding area on the north bank, the East End of the City of London.

Memories of the life and death struggle in which they had been personally involved as children were still vivid and they recounted their stories with great feeling, like the night when molten sugar ran down the streets after the Tate and Lyle sugar refinery was hit. They woke to find streets closed because buildings had been destroyed by the bombing and would return home from working in the City each evening not knowing if their homes would still be standing or their neighbours still alive.

The famous Arsenal Football Club originated in the nearby town of Woolwich where the Royal Arsenal, with its various armaments factories was located. When we arrived the optical works, where telescopic gun sightings had once been made, still stood on a site near to the church. The Royal Engineers were based nearby and early Superintendents of the Slade Mission, as it was first called, bore the ranks of Majors and Captains.

Our new church family

Our children loved their new home and immediately threw themselves into the youth activities of the church. I felt an immediate sense of relief at having a group of experienced leaders around me and Val and I came to realise just how lonely our first experience of church leadership had been.

The three bed semi-detached house that was first

> Molten sugar ran down the streets after the Tate and Lyle sugar refinery was hit.

> Its people are splashed across the canvas of my memory like an abstract painting full of vivid colours.

provided for us was a vast improvement on our Willesden maisonette but we were very grateful when a much more spacious property became available and we quickly settled in and made it our home.

The church was already so well established that Val was not expected to take up the leadership of women's meetings or any other responsibilities that might otherwise be expected of a Minister's wife. That left her free to focus on caring for the family and gradually find her way into the church at her own pace. She soon made firm friends in whom she could confide and who watched over her so that, when she experienced a second period of severe illness, they were there to support her and our family.

Unlike any other church

The Slade is unlike any other church we have ever known. It reflects the rich cultural tapestry of the area from which the congregation is gathered. The uninhibited behaviour, language and attitudes of some of its people are splashed across the canvas of my memory like an abstract painting full of vivid colours. We often found ourselves wondering and despairing within the space of an hour; wondering at the amazing devotion, grace and sensitivity displayed by many of our people, despairing at the unpredictable and sometimes outrageous behaviour of the few.

No day was dull. The neighbourhood seemed to be full of gritty people with little room for sentimentality and unreality. We generally found this to be very endearing and grew to love the people in the church very much. Their straightforward openness was usually refreshing and their readiness to laugh at pretension or stupidity of any kind made for solid relationships.

It meant that I also could be direct and straightforward with them and sometimes a lasting friendship emerged from a bruising first encounter.

Enormous changes took place over the twelve years we were at The Slade. The congregation increased and changed as new people came and elderly long-time members died. The building was refurbished and the Brigades were replaced, leaders retired and a younger generation stepped up to take its turn in leading the church and an increasingly multicultural community began to make its impact.

But the essential character of the congregation remained the same, lively and cheeky, warm and open, whole-hearted in devotion to Christ and courageous in reaching out to the local community and beyond.

When the time came for us to leave we knew that we were unlikely ever to experience again a church like The Slade. Whatever legacy we may have left behind in the hearts of the people, the church made an indelible impression on us and, whenever we remember the people and recount our adventures there, we find ourselves smiling and being grateful for the experiences that taught us so much.

Chapter 47
WIDENING HORIZONS

After eight years as a solo Pastor, the church agreed to employ a second minister to work alongside me.

Andrew Paterson had a rich church heritage, both his father and grandfather being prominent ministers. He was a gifted and able man who, although with us for only two years, added a new dimension to our efforts to develop the church. With him present to lead in our absence, we seized the opportunity to take a sabbatical break, the first in eighteen years.

At this time I also became more involved in the activities of the association of Churches to which The Slade belonged, The Fellowship of Independent Evangelical Churches, FIEC.

From local to national church work
Formed in 1922, the founders of FIEC had the vision to link and serve the hundreds of independent churches, chapels and missions which had sprung up throughout the UK. Many of them were thriving but they were isolated and disadvantaged by their somewhat solitary existence.

However, gathering fiercely independent

churches into an association proved to be a little like herding cats. Many, having already withdrawn from denominations that had moved away from historic orthodox Biblical Christianity, had an inbuilt aversion to joining anything. It is to their credit that the first leaders of the Fellowship persisted in their vison so that, by the end of the 1980's, FIEC had over four hundred churches affiliated to it and at its height its annual gathering attracted over three thousand church representatives and members.

An appeal by the General Secretary for younger ministers to become more involved encouraged me to accept invitations to join various committees which often met in Westminster Chapel, near Buckingham Palace in central London. I found it stimulating to meet older, more experienced men and to hear them debate issues of the day and I later welcomed the invitation to become a member of FIEC's National Council. Some of those who had been its foremost architects had by this time died and their immediate successors were elderly and facing challenges which did not exist in the early days.

After nearly seventy years, enthusiasm for FIEC among the churches was on the wane and resources were drying up. The time had come to re-examine what role, if any, it had in the contemporary church scene in Britain. It was a critical time for the Council and its natural conservatism meant that a successful outcome to its discussions was by no means assured.

However, following a thorough review of the British evangelical landscape, the Council became convinced that no other body was doing precisely what FIEC was doing for independent churches and found very good reasons for rescuing it for generations to come.

By this time I was heavily involved with others in drawing up plans for its renewal and when, in

1990, the time came to appoint someone to travel the British Isles to take proposals to the churches and collect their responses, I was invited by the Council to take on the task. So I resigned my position at The Slade and Val and I together committed ourselves to touring the country for a year. Generously, The Slade agreed that we could remain in the manse while I carried out that task.

❝❝They took advantage of the rare opportunity to unburden themselves to trustworthy strangers.

An unforgettable journey

Our journey around the churches proved to be a fascinating education for us both. We bought a small touring caravan with which we criss-crossed the country and, while I addressed dozens of meetings of ministers and elders of churches from Scotland to Southampton and from Exeter to Norwich, Val kept home in our cosy mobile haven.

We met, and were humbled by, many hard working and dedicated church leaders whose devotion to Christ and to making him known in their community was inspiring. We shared their enthusiasm for new ventures and delighted in stories of people won for Christ. And we listened for hours as they took advantage of the rare opportunity to unburden themselves to trustworthy strangers.

They told of their loneliness in ministry and of their personal struggles, of their hopes and fears for the churches they led. We were deeply affected by those conversations and my subsequent report to the Council not only featured many statistics and the opinions of church leaders, but also a heartfelt account of their loneliness and vulnerability to discouragement.

The Council responded positively to our findings and, with the support of the churches, duly implemented a new vision which did much to revive the Fellowship over the next decade.

It has gone through many changes since that time so that today it numbers over five hundred churches and is part of a greatly expanded network of relationships between evangelical churches and church bodies both here in the UK and also elsewhere in the world, but those years of rebuilding the Fellowship remain indelibly etched on my memory.

At the end of that year The Slade needed the manse in which we were living to house its new minister and his family, and I needed to find new employment. We had been so touched by the need of the churches and their leaders that Val and I agreed that, if there was any way of continuing to serve them, we should be willing for that.

And so it transpired. The Council extended its invitation to me to continue my work for a further three years helping to implement the new vision. So, one year became three and three eventually became fourteen years on staff with FIEC. I became its General Secretary, the senior executive staff member, in 1999, a position I held until 2004 when our lives took another direction altogether.

Escape to the country

The day we left Plumstead and headed out of London for the last time came as a huge relief to Val. For the first time in thirty years of married life we would choose somewhere to live in the English West Country, our home area, and have the liberty to select a property we loved. We would no longer be in the goldfish bowl of local church leadership and she could at last spend time doing the things she loved most, reading, writing – and researching my history.

While she relished her quieter, more private life, mine became more demanding. With the increasing use of technology I was able to work from home and have a secretary to assist me.

I was regularly away from home, sometimes in our main office in Croydon, just south of London, but also in various committee rooms around the capital or travelling to the far reaches of the British Isles to visit churches that needed support. Occasionally I also represented FIEC abroad.

It was a demanding role with many challenges, but working with leading Ministers within the evangelical world at that time was a privilege, an education and a revelation to me of the way in which they thought and how they approached the work of the ministry. I learned much from them and many of them became very good friends.

Chapter 48
OUT OF LEFT FIELD

It was in 2003 that Val and I first began to sense that my work with FIEC was coming to an end. It's hard to explain how that came about but over the ensuing year, by degrees, my roots were loosened and, although physically still quite fit, at 63 years of age I became aware that a new wind was blowing and a rising generation needed younger leadership to inspire it if the progress that had been made was to continue. And there was a very good man in the wings who was waiting to be my successor.

The timing was not particularly good for us since I would not receive my pension until the summer of 2005, but we were sufficiently restless to take time out to talk and pray about our future.

We skipped church one beautiful summer Sunday in June 2004 and found a secluded meadow in the glorious grounds of Bowood House, a grade I listed Georgian country house near Chippenham in Wiltshire. There we sat with our picnic and talked, read and prayed until the sun began to set and it was time for the grounds to close to the public.

This was her time
Early on in our discussion I told Val that, whatever

❝ Whatever our future might be, I wanted this to be 'her time'

our future might be, I wanted this to be 'her time'. After a lifetime of supporting me so faithfully and enduring situations that were very challenging for her, I wanted to give back to her as much as I could of the lost opportunities to be together and to enjoy our six grandchildren. I would be dedicated to making her retirement as enjoyable, restful and satisfying as possible.

By the end of the day we were agreed that, as a first step, I should resign my position in FIEC and, if no other opening presented itself, I would contact a major store chain that was advertising jobs for mature people to see what employment might be available locally. I fondly imagined that it would be a relief for us both if I did something routine, even monotonous for a few months. But we were soon to discover that retirement would be far more elusive than that.

So why don't you come then?

The very next day our close friend, Colin Smith, arrived from America. We had been expecting him because he had been booked for 2 years to speak at the 10th Anniversary of a course we had put together to train church leaders, although he had not featured in our conversation at all the previous day. It was not long before we learned that he was troubled by something that had happened just before he left home the previous day.

The 2000 strong church that Colin led in the NW suburbs of Chicago was in the final stages of appointing an Executive Pastor to work beside him but the appointment had unexpectedly fallen through. It didn't make sense. The candidate, a mutual friend, was eminently qualified for the role. He had met with the church leaders who were simply expecting to sign off on the appointment but frustratingly the meeting didn't go well. Plans that had been laid over some months now lay in tatters and Colin could see no way forward.

We listened and sympathised with his dilemma and, when at length he asked about our situation, we shared with him the decision we had made the day before his arrival.

That evening I drove him to an engagement some distance from our home and as we journeyed our conversation continued. Just as I pulled into the drive of the house where he would be staying, he suddenly said, "So why don't you come then?" This was completely out of left field and we both laughed at the idea. It didn't take long for me to point out the problems with the suggestion. "Of course I would love to work with you, my friend", I said, "but only yesterday we made plans to be nearer our family and retire. Even if you could persuade me to join you, it would be a step too far for Val. This is her time and I have promised to give her the chance to choose what we do. Surely common sense says that it is too late for us to be doing anything of the sort."

When I arrived home that night I said to Val, "You will never guess what Colin has suggested!" She replied, "I know exactly what he has suggested and here are the reasons why it can't happen." She was right in every respect. It was a crazy idea that at our time of life, after her years of illness and when we both needed a quieter life to enjoy our retirement and our grandchildren, we should agree to be 4000 miles from them in a strange culture. As we laughed at the idea I said, "We don't need to be too concerned. I can't believe that Colin was serious." How wrong I was!

I went to bed and slept soundly, but Val didn't. She wrestled in prayer and argued her way through the night in conversation with Christ. And He spoke

> I thought I heard you say that you would be willing to do anything I asked of you. What has changed?

to her. "What was it you said only yesterday? I thought I heard you say that you would be willing to do anything I asked of you. What has changed? Are you really not willing to consider serving me in Chicago?" It was as clear as that to her.

Next morning she called me out of my office. "We have to think about this," she said. I was bemused by this change of heart, "Who is this woman?" I said. But this was her time and I was keen to hear what she had to say.

Despite her many years of suffering and vulnerability, Val began to believe that it was after all God's will for us to consider another adventure, this time in another part of the world altogether and, once she was convinced that it was God who was speaking to us, the issue was settled. There was nothing for it, we had to follow his lead.

This was her time for sure, but she could think of no better use of that time than to be in the very centre of God's will, whatever that meant.

Telling the family

One of the key considerations in working through the process of making the decision was our concern for our family. The pattern of my working life, and Val's ongoing vulnerability, meant that we had all too few opportunities to meet and relate closely to our children and grandchildren. We fondly imagined that retirement would allow us to claw back some lost time with them and so we planned to move somewhere nearer to them when the time was right.

After some weeks of internet and telephone exchanges with the church in Chicago, it was time to share this unexpected turn of events with our three families before we made a final decision.

We were keen for them to understand how the invitation had come about and why we had an increasing sense that we must go. We wanted them to know that we loved them and that leaving them was not at all easy for us. In fact, one of our greatest concerns was that by moving to the USA we would forfeit the opportunity to be there for them and influence our grandchildren for Christ. Not one of our children was following Him at that time. How could we possibly leave them now?

Ian and Kate and their families were shocked at the news. "People of your age don't do things like this," they said. "It's for the young." But as the conversation moved on and they could see that we were convinced that God was leading us – and that a new foreign holiday destination was looming into sight, they decided that it was not altogether a bad thing.

Our visit to Philip the other side of London would be more testing. He would be rigorous in his assessment of our plans. After explaining the situation as briefly as we could, he said nothing so I kept talking. I came at least to share our concerns for the family, particularly focusing on the fact that we longed for him, Ian and Kate to return to faith in Jesus Christ and, if we answered the invitation of the church in Chicago positively, we were keenly aware that we would have fewer opportunities to share our lives with them and their children.

By now I expected him to interrupt and say as he had on a previous occasion, "Don't get too heavy, Dad." But he still said nothing. So I set off again and this time he did interrupt. I shall never forget his words. As we reflected on them later they seemed to be words from Christ Himself that clinched our conviction that He was guiding us.

"Nothing could be further from the truth, Dad." We were rocked back on our heels. "What do you mean?" I asked. Then slowly the story came out.

Six months earlier Philip, Jessica and the boys had
attended their school's Christmas carol service in
a local Anglican Church. The service itself was not
particularly memorable but they decided that they
would go back to the church to see what it was like
and, when they did, they were sufficiently impressed
to continue to attend.

It turned out to be a well-known Anglican
evangelical church with faithful preaching and a
lively congregation of believers in our Lord Jesus
Christ. After a short while Philip's faith was restored
and later Jessica, too, came to profess faith in Christ.
We knew nothing of this until this moment when we
most needed confirmation that what we were doing
was from God and, just in case we had missed the
point, Philip added, "God did this without you, Dad.
So you can go. It's OK." It was shocking – but he was
right.

New life – new challenges

Barely four months after our day of reflection and
prayer and our first conversation with Colin, with all
our belongings sold and our house let, we flew into
Chicago O'Hare airport on our way to a new life, a
life to which undoubtedly the Lord had led us.

In the months that followed when Val faced radical
surgery on two occasions and her terminal illness
began to take its toll, she received the best of medical
attention and the comfort of a huge and generous
congregation that poured out its love on us both, and
despite everything I saw her happier than she had
been for many years. As her body weakened, her
faith seemed to grow ever stronger as she prepared
to meet Christ at last. This was her time. She lived
sacrificially to the end but was no poorer for that.
Rather she entered into the presence of the Lord she
loved and received that unimaginable reward that he

had always planned to give her.

And she left me one last precious gift. She made it clear to me, and to our children, that after she had gone she wanted me to marry again. "He won't be good on his own," she said to Kate through her tears. And three years later I did, to Ann, with whom I have found happiness again.

He won't be good on his own.

Chapter 49
I'M GLAD YOU ASKED

When I tell my story, those who listen always have many questions. Most concern details of the narrative. They focus on clarifying some part of the complicated details of the story. But I'm always most interested in those questions that probe the deeper issues that arise in relation to my experience as a Christian.

There are two issues that people raise most often, questions that relate to the subject of forgiveness and those that concern the seeming conflict between the sad things that happened to me and my conviction that my life has always been in the hands of a gracious and caring God.

Forgiveness

As for the question of forgiveness – as Val began to uncover the truth about my early childhood she quietly became outraged on my behalf at the way I had been treated and wondered if deep down I also felt the same way. If so, why had I never mentioned it or shown it? Maybe it was simply that I had never looked at my history in any detail before she laid it all out, or perhaps I was simply in denial.

Other people have probed that same issue. "Don't

> **How damaging bitterness and resentment, self-pity or a quest for revenge can be. It's a dead end.**

you feel any bitterness towards those who treated you as they did? Whatever you say, you were a victim and suffered for it at the time and have lived with the consequences ever since. It would be only natural for you to feel at least a little resentful. If you are indifferent to what happened does that mean that you are out of touch with your feelings?" Let me answer it as honestly as I know how.

By nature I have always been a forward-looking person who anticipates what is coming rather than navigating life through the rear view mirror. That may be something I learned as a way of escape from the past, I don't know. However, in my work as a Pastor for over 50 years I have had plenty of opportunity to observe just how damaging bitterness and resentment, self-pity or a quest for revenge can be. It's a dead end and anyway, in my case, entirely inappropriate. How can I spend time and energy focused on the bad behaviour of other people when I have been forgiven so much and have been loved so much by God Himself and also by those who know him?

As I write, the death of Jill Saward has just been announced. She was 51 years of age. Jill was brutally raped in 1986 during a robbery at her father's vicarage in Ealing, West London. She was the first victim of sexual assault in the UK to waive her right to anonymity so that she could lead a campaign against sexual crimes, a campaign that transformed public attitudes and led to changes in the law. Her courage in dealing with her trauma, and her willingness to forgive and even to meet one of her attackers, stands as a lasting testimony to her devotion to Christ and the freedom he brings to his people.

When her husband was questioned about her willingness to forgive, he explained that as a couple they were committed to love and justice. Forgiveness is not about letting people off or pretending that nothing serious has happened. It is about releasing personal bitterness and anger, refusing to allow that terrible event to dictate their outlook and dominate their lives. Then he quoted the Lord's Prayer where it says, "… forgive us our debts, as we also have forgiven our debtors."*

And that's the point. God's forgiveness obliges, motivates and empowers those who know Him to forgive and to find release in the process.

I also believe in justice and recognise its importance for a well ordered society and for our life in relation to God. However, justice is frequently elusive in this world and many terrible crimes go unsolved and unpunished. It is natural for us to cry out for justice and God hears such prayers and has appointed a Judge and a day of accounting when He, with unerring wisdom, will summon all people who have every lived to answer to Him.

So I am called to leave all judgement to Him who alone sees everything with absolute clarity and has the power to judge, to condemn and to forgive. Our human systems of justice have their place, of that there is no doubt, and must be upheld, but Christ's final judgement will address all injustice perfectly. A story that Jesus told settles the issue for me.

A king called his servants to account. One owed him such a huge amount that there was no way he could possibly repay him. The king ordered that he and his family be sold into slavery to repay the debt but, such was the intensity of the servant's appeal for time and clemency, the king forgave him everything.

However, that same servant went out and found a fellow servant who owed him very little and, despite his desperate appeal, the forgiven servant refused to forgive and had the debtor imprisoned until he could

> Is it reasonable to believe that there is a good God who created all things and who is concerned with each individual and the details of their life?

repay what he owed.

When the king heard about it he condemned the servant he had forgiven, rescinded his decision and put him prison under harsh conditions. Jesus ends the story with these words, "This is how my heavenly Father will treat each of you unless you forgive your brother from your heart."*

Bad experiences and a gracious God

What about the seeming conflict between the bad things that happened to me and to Val and our conviction that our life has been in the hands of a good and caring God all the time?

This is a common and often agonising issue to deal with. It is expressed in various ways usually when suffering, disappointment or grief engulf us. Theologians refer to 'the mystery of God's providence'. It conjures up images of people in anguish struggling to make sense of a tragedy that has overtaken them. "Why has this happened to me? Is there any rhyme or reason to life under the sun? If only I could understand why this has happened, I may find hope again and some way through my misery."

Behind our personal pain and questioning lies another question that is equally challenging. Is it reasonable to believe that there is a good God who created all things and that he is concerned with each individual and the details of their life?

Cambridge's renowned Professor, 72 year old Stephen Hawking, is a theoretical physicist, cosmologist and author. I gather that he is frequently asked if science can prove that God does not exist. His reply is to the effect that, 'since the human race is just chemical scum on a moderate-sized planet, orbiting around a very average star in the outer suburbs of one among a hundred billion galaxies, we are so insignificant that I can't believe the whole universe exists for our benefit. It is difficult to believe in a god who would care about us or even notice our existence.'

> **It is a mistake to confuse size with value.**

If he is right that the idea of a caring God is absurd, we have every reason to consider Christians hopelessly ego-centric and unsophisticated, a people to be pitied for inventing a god to make them feel safe and to support them in their lonely, meaningless journey through this world.

But it is a mistake to confuse size with value. The toddler who is given an expensive present on Christmas day may be forgiven for finding more pleasure in the box in which it came than in the gift which holds promise of years of enjoyment. We should not do the same, '… worshipping created things rather than the Creator – who is for ever praised'.*

It's worth pointing out that this is not a new question invented by modern science. A thousand years before Christ was born, the shepherd boy, David, who became Israel's greatest king, wrote of how he pondered exactly the same question. He spent many a long night out under clear starlit skies and wrote in wonder at what he witnessed and the impact it made on him.

"When I consider your heavens, the work of your fingers, the moon and the stars, which you have set in place, what is man that you are mindful of him, the son of man that you care for him?"**

Interestingly, after Christ had come and returned to heaven, the apostle Paul addresses the same issue in a slightly different way when he writes to the church in Ephesus in the first century AD.

"… I pray that you … may have the power … to grasp how wide and long and high and deep is the love of Christ, and to know this love that surpasses

> **The way he made us and what he did for us confirms that human beings have value above all creation.**

knowledge …"* In other words, for anyone to grasp that the God of all creation loves them personally, it is necessary for the power of God himself to reveal it to them and so give them the capacity to appreciate what is otherwise impossible to grasp.

Stephen Hawking is amazed that not more of us study the stars. Many of us who live in towns and cities live largely under the canopy of artificial light and are seldom able to view the heavens from a place of complete darkness. That view, unrestricted by artificial light, has the power to bring perspective to our existence on this earth and our place in the scheme of things. But if we only observe the stars without looking through them, beyond them, they may do no more than make us feel inconsequential 'chemical scum', momentarily passing through this world with no point or purpose to our existence.

In contrast to that David writes, "You have set your glory above the heavens. From the lips of children and infants you have ordained praise … you made (human kind) a little lower than the heavenly beings and crowned him with glory and honour."**

The God who made all things has chosen to create human beings quite unlike all other creatures. He says that we are made in some ways like our Creator and for a relationship with Him. In addition, when we chose to rebel against Him, of his own free will and because he would love us, He came in the Person of Jesus Christ to live, die and be raised from the dead for our salvation and for reconciliation, God with us and we with Him.

The way he made us and what he did for us confirms that human beings have value above all creation so, far from being arrogant to believe in God's personal care for us, it is in fact the height of human arrogance to reject his version of events simply because our minds cannot comprehend Him or fathom His ways.

So my answer to the question of how I account for the seeming disparity between my belief in God's love for me, and the hard experiences through which I have passed, is precisely the same as every generation of Christian believers before me and those who will come after me. I cannot tell you why God planned my life as he did, but if He could place such value on me by sending the Lord Jesus Christ, His own Son, to die for me, and watch over me all these years, then I know he planned in love and has shaped me through the trials and the joys of life for my ultimate and eternal benefit.

> *"To whom will you compare me? Or who is my equal?" says the Holy One.*
> *Lift up your eyes and look to the heavens. Who created all these?*
> *He brings out the starry host one by one, and calls them each by name.*
> *Because of his great power and mighty strength, not one of them is missing...*
> *Do you not know?*
> *Have you not heard?*
> *The Lord is the everlasting God, the Creator of the ends of the earth.*
> *He will not grow tired or weary, and his understanding no-one can fathom.*
> *He gives strength to the weary and increases the power of the weak.*
> *Even youths grow tired and weary, and young men stumble and fall,*
> *But those who hope in the Lord will renew their strength.*
> *They will soar on wings like eagles,*
> *They will run and not grow weary,*
> *They will walk and not be faint."**

*Isa 40:25ff

EPILOGUE

Much to my surprise, at 60 years of age there seemed no alternative but for me to search for my human roots. It had to be. The compulsion to discover the truth about my past and maybe to find even the shadow of a relationship with those who gave me life, gradually built in me until it became irresistible.

How much of that was because of Val's enthusiasm, and how much was the pressure of my own needs, is impossible for me to say, but there is no doubting the fact that the experience, and the record of the search, has left me in a different place. It has been an education, a revelation, an awakening that has impacted me deeply. It was often fascinating, deeply disturbing and puzzling but seldom dull. I now know my history and have pretty much laid the past to rest.

But one thing remains clear to me. This journey has changed very little that is fundamentally important to me. In fact, it has served only to confirm what I have known since I was young, that even before I was born, God, for reasons I will never understand, planned to watch over me, make me his child and be good to me. 'Somebody's Son' became a child of God and that relationship changed my life and destiny completely. "I know that I find who I am in Jesus Christ, not in genetics. My identity in Him never changes …"